COMPUTER

NETWORKING

BEGINNERS GUIDE:

Networking for beginners. A Simple

and Easy guide to manage a Network

Computer System from the Basics

ERICK STACK

Table of Contents

Introduction 6

Chapter 1. IP Addresses and Configuration............................... 14

How the Internet is Connected?.. 23

Basic Components of Computer Network 24

Computer Network Hardware System 24

How the Internet is given to people?...27

Internet Communications..27

Mobile Communications... 28

LTE and Voice Call.. 28

Chapter 2. Wireless hardware and standard 30

Chapter 3. Wireless Technologies... 43

Components of a wireless network 44

Setting up a wireless network 46

Factors to consider when installing a large wireless network................ 48

Chapter 4. Managing Routers and Switches 51

Remote Administration 51

Managing Configurations 55

Factory Defaults..59

Upgrading Cisco IOS.. 62

Chapter 5. Advanced Configurations 65

Dynamic Host Configuration Protocol (DHCP) 65

Chapter 6. IPv6 vs IPv4 .... **68**

Chapter 7. The Internet's big arena **73**

Once upon the time... .... *73*

Internet services *75*

Chapter 8. Subnetting Basics **77**

Chapter 9. Subnetting Examples **89**

How to determine a subnet address? *89*

How to determine the number of bits to borrow from the hosts for subnetting? *93*

Subnetting with Class A address *94*

Subnetting with class B address *97*

Subnetting with class C address *103*

Chapter 10. IPv6 Subnetting **107**

Hex conversions for fun *110*

Chapter 11. Scaling Networks **113**

Chapter 12. How to Secure Your Network **126**

Update your patches *126*

Configure your exception handling processes *127*

Conduct assurance processes *127*

Use strong passwords *128*

Secure your VPN *134*

Implement Access Control *135*

Data loss prevention *136*

Use antimalware and antivirus software *138*

Wireless security *138*

Network Segmentation *139*

Intrusion Prevention System *140*

Email security *140*

Web Security *140*

Application Security *141*

Behavioral Analytics *141*

Consider physical network security *142*

Wireless Network Security *143*

Conclusion **145**

Introduction

A computer network connects mobile phones, computers, It devices, and peripherals. Routers, Switches, and wireless access points are some of the essential networking basics. These basics allow devices that are connected to a network to communicate effectively with one another and, if necessary, with other networks such as the Internet.

Routers, Switches, and wireless access points

These three networking devices perform different but related functions that make a network what it is. Without their input, there wouldn't be a network.

Switches

Most of business networks are built on switches. A networking switch connects computers, a controller, servers, and printers to a network within a location. Switches allow the connected devices on a network to communicate smoothly and efficiently with each other. They can also communicate with other networks and thus create a network where resources can be shared in the process. Through resource allocation and information sharing, switches increase productivity and also save money.

There are two types of switches for computer networking: managed and unmanaged switches.

• Managed switches: A managed switch is a switch that can be configured. You can easily monitor a managed switch as well as adjust it either remotely or locally. This gives you absolute control over network access and traffic.

• Unmanaged switches: The unmanaged switches are used mostly for small businesses. They are mostly used for managing data flow between a single device or a couple of computers.

• Enterprise: Enterprise switches are the ideal for large companies that have tiers of networks for controlling and monitoring a whole network simultaneously. The enterprise switches are by far the most powerful and equally the most expensive.

• Smart type: This switch combines the properties of both the managed and unmanaged switches. They are capable of making changes to the settings of a network, an action that may have a huge impact on the system's settings.

Routers

Routers play a very significant role in a network. When a couple of networks are to be connected together, routers are assigned that task. If there are computers on the connected networks, these will be connected to the Internet too. Thus, routers give room to all computers that are already networked to use a single source of Internet connection, saving the consumer's money.

A router can also assume the role of a catcher by analyzing the data sent across to a network, selecting the best route for data transfer, and completing its roles by sending the data via the chosen route. If you're a businessman, routers are on hand to connect your business to all four corners of the world. It also protects your information from both internal and external security threats. When necessary, a router will assign computers order of priority over each other. Aside from the basic networking functions that routers are known for, they are equipped with some other features that increase the security of networking as well as make it easier.

Depending on why you want to use a router, you can choose from the different types of routers, including an Internet Protocol (IP), those with a virtual private network (VPN), or a firewall.

Access points

An access point also has a distinct role that combines with the functions of the other components to make networking a reality. Access points allows wireless connection of devices to a wireless network. The elimination of cables allows new devices to be brought online in addition to offering mobile workers flexible support. An access point also takes the role of an amplifier for a network. It is true that the router is the one that provides the bandwidth, but the access point takes it up from there. It extends the provided bandwidth to support the network's ability to support more devices. These devices can now access the network from wherever they are, even if they are farther away.

The job of an access point doesn't stop at extending bandwidth. An access point can also provide valuable data about the connected devices on a network in addition to providing proactive security for the network. It can also serve any other valuable practical purposes as needed by the network. Access points have a reputation for supporting a wide range of IEEE standards. Each of the supported standards is a ratified amendment as deemed fit by the regulatory body. These standards don't operate on a single frequency but on different frequencies. They also support different channels as well as deliver diverse bandwidth.

Hubs

A hub ranks high among the basic networking devices. It is used exclusively for connecting a number of computers or some other networked devices such as mobile phones together to a single source of Internet connection. For instance, a computer can be connected to a printer, server, and another computer via a network hub.

Unlike a router or a switch, a hub has no intelligence or routing tables where it can send information and transfer all network data to all the connections on a network. In recent times, though, wireless technologies are gradually becoming the order of the day. With Wi-Fi and Bluetooth taking over, hubs are now used in wireless applications. It is not surprising, then, that Wi-Fi and

Bluetooth enabled phones can easily connect to a single hub with wired connections.

A hub is a huge power consumer and needs a regular power supply for it to effectively provide the best service. This places a huge responsibility on its user who must ensure that it doesn't lack the appropriate power supply that it needs to function effectively.

A typical example of a simple hub is the USB hub. This hub allows a computer to accept connection from multiple USB devices, although the computer itself may not have sufficient USB connections for such a huge number of USB devices. This should give you an idea of how a hub works, even in networking.

There are three types of networking hubs. These are:

•   Active hubs: This is a type of networking hub that doesn't work only as a connector but regenerates any incoming signal before it transmits them. This is to ensure that the received signals are strong. The active hub is also known as a multiport repeater. It is not satisfied with the role of a simple interface in networking but actively participates in the networking as well. It also takes an active part in data communication by the strong signals it receives via the input ports before it eventually forwards them.

An active hub can also closely monitor any data it forwards and occasionally helps to improve the signal before it forwards the data to the recipients: other connections. This awesome feature is a big help while troubleshooting network problems as it makes troubleshooting easier and faster.

• Passive hubs: The passive hub acts only as a pass-through and doesn't regenerate incoming signals it receives via its input port. It transmits them through its output port as it receives them. Thus, unlike the active hub, it doesn't participate in the networking but only acts as a connector for a couple of wires in a networking topology.

• Intelligent hubs: An intelligent hub is a multipurpose networking hub that can play the roles of both the active and passive hubs efficiently. It can also assist in the management of the network resources to boost the overall performance of a network.

During troubleshooting, this hub will come pretty handy. It can pinpoint the actual location of whatever problem you encounter during network and equally assist with identifying the root cause of the problem as well as proffer solutions to it.

An intelligent hub can perform some other functions such as routing, bridging, network management, and switching.

Bridges

A network bridge is another important networking tool. A bridge, just as its name implies, connects two separate computer networks with the aim of enabling them to communicate. It also allows the connected computer networks to come together and work, not as independent networks, but a single network.

Bridges are commonly used for extending the reach of networks, most especially, in Local Area Networks (LANs). This allows the LAN to cover larger areas than it can otherwise reach without the input of a bridge. Bridges share some similarities with repeaters, although they are more intelligent. A network bridge will inspect any incoming network traffic critically to enable it to determine whether it should transfer the traffic to the network or discard it. It uses the intended destination of the traffic to determine what to do with it. For instance, an Ethernet bridge will inspect all incoming Ethernet frames one after the other, including the source of the frame as well as its destination MAC addresses when making decisions about forwarding.

Chapter 1.   IP Addresses and Configuration

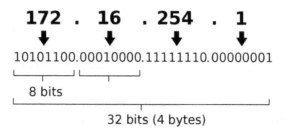

IPv4 address in dotted-decimal notation

172 . 16 . 254 . 1

10101100.00010000.11111110.00000001

8 bits

32 bits (4 bytes)

Computers and other devices on a network use IP addresses to communicate with each other. MAC (media access control) addresses are also used for network communication, but that's a story for another day!

An IP address is a number (for the sake of simplicity) that is assigned to a computer that is then used to communicate with other computers and devices that also have an IP address assigned to them. It consists of four sets of numbers (called octets) and looks something like this – 192.168.10.240. There are several types of address classes, and things can get really complicated, so I will just stick with the basics so you have an understanding of how IP addresses are used. For now, we are mostly using IPv4, but soon will be using IPv6 since we are out of public version 4 addresses.

When you want to connect to another computer on the network (or even to a website), you can type in its name, and then a service called DNS (Domain Name System) translates that computer or website name into the IP address of that computer or web server. That way you don't have to memorize IP addresses and only need to know the computer name or website name. On a network, you can't have the same IP address assigned to two devices otherwise there will be a conflict.

There are also what is known as public and private IP addresses. Public IP addresses are used for things such as web servers, and are unique to that server (meaning that IP address can't be used on any other public\Internet device in the world). Private IP addresses, on the other hand, can be used by anyone on their internal network and assigned to devices that only communicate with other internal devices. That doesn't mean these internal devices can't connect to the Internet or other public devices. To do this, the private IP address is translated to a public IP address through the process of NAT (Network Address Translation), which is usually done on your router. This process is beyond the scope of this book, but feel free to look it up if you want to learn more about it.

So, the bottom line is that your computer needs an IP address to communicate on the network, and even to get on the Internet. There are a few ways to find the IP address of your computer, and I will now go over what I think is the easiest one. If you open a command prompt (which is a way to run text based commands on your computer like they did before Windows), you can type in a certain command to find your IP address information. The Complete Picture of the Web

Let's first take a look at the full picture of how a browser accesses a Web server. The process of accessing a Web server and displaying a Web page involves a series of interactions between the Browser and the Web server, primarily the following.

(1) Browser: "Please give me the web page data. "

(2) Web

(2) Web Server: "Ok will do it"

After this series of interactions is complete, the browser displays the data it receives from the Web server on the screen. While the process of displaying a web page is complex, the interaction between the browser and the server over the network is surprisingly simple. When we shop in an online mall, we type in the name of the product and the address of the goods we want to receive and send it to a Web server.

(1) Browser: "please process these order data. "

(2) Web

(2) Web Server: "okay, Order Data received.

While the actual processing of an order with the sales system after the Web server receives the order data is complex, the interaction between the Browser and the Web server is simple, as summarized below.

(1) the browser sends a request to the Web server.

(2) Web

(3) The Web server sends a response to the browser based on the request.

So at this level, where Web applications like browsers and Web servers interact, it should be relatively easy to understand how it works. The interaction at this level is very similar to the dialogue between humans and is easier to understand from this point 1.

To enable interaction between applications, we need a mechanism to pass requests and responses between the Browser and the Web server. The network is composed of many computers and other devices connected to each other, so in the process of communication, we need to determine the correct communication object and send the request and response to them. Requests and responses can be lost or corrupted during delivery, so these situations must also be considered. So we need a mechanism to send requests and responses to each other without fail, no matter what the situation. Since the request and response are both 0 and 1 pieces of digital information, it can be said that we need a mechanism to carry the digital information to the designated destination.

This mechanism is implemented by the network control software in the operating system, as well as the division of labor between switches, routers and other devices. Its basic idea is to divide the digital information into small pieces It is then shipped in containers called "packs". The word "Bag" is a word that you may often come across when using a mobile phone, but here it is similar to the concept used in postal and courier services.

You can think of a package as a letter or package, and a switch or router as a sorting area for a post office or a delivery company. The header of the packet contains the destination information, which can be sorted according to the relay of many switches and routers, and then carried to the destination step by step. Whether it's a home and corporate LAN, or the Internet out there, they're just different in size, and the underlying mechanisms are the same.

Together with Web applications such as browsers and Web servers, these two parts of the Web make up the Web. That is to say, these two parts are put together, the whole picture of the network.

We'll start by exploring how the browser works. You can think of our exploration as starting with typing a URL into your browser. Of course, the browser is not personally responsible for the transfer of data. The mechanism that carries the digital information is responsible for sending the message, so the browser delegates the data to it. Specifically, the network control software in the operating system is delegated to send messages to the server.

One of the first to appear is the protocol stack (network control software called Protocol Stack). The software packages the messages it receives from the browser and adds control information such as the destination address. To use the post office analogy is to put the letter in an envelope and write the addressee's address on the envelope.

The software also has other functions, such as resending packets in the event of a communication error or adjusting the rate at which data is sent, perhaps we can think of it as a little secretary who helps us send letters.

Next, the stack hands the packet to the network card (the hardware responsible for Ethernet or wireless network communications). The Network Card then converts the packet into an electrical signal and sends it out over the wire. In this way, the packet enters the network.

What comes next will vary according to the form of Internet access. A client computer can access the Internet either through a home or corporate Lan or directly on its own. Unfortunately, our exploration does not cover all of these possibilities, so we have to assume, for example, that the client computer is connected to a home or Corporate Lan Then through ADSL and fiber to the home (FTTH) and other broadband lines to access the Internet.

In such a scenario, packets sent by a network card pass through a switch or other device to a router used to access the Internet. Behind the router is the Internet, and the network operator is responsible for delivering the package to the destination, just as the postman is responsible for delivering the letter to the recipient after we drop it into the mailbox.

The data then travels from the router used to access the Internet to the inside of the Internet. The gateway to the Internet is called the access network. In general, we can use telephone lines, Isdn, Adsl, cable television, light, private lines, and other communication lines to access the Internet, these communication lines collectively known as an access network. An access network connects to a contracted network operator and to a device called a Point of Presence (PoP).

The entity of the access point is a router designed for the operator, which we can think of as the nearest post office to your home. Letters collected from various mailboxes are sorted at post offices and then sent around the country or even around the world, as is the case with the Internet, where packets are first sent through an access network to an access point and then sent from here to the rest of the country and the world. Behind the access point is the backbone of the Internet.

There are many operators and a large number of routers in the backbone network. These routers are connected to each other to form a huge network, and our network packet is passed through the relay of several routers Is eventually sent to the target Web server. The details are explained in the main text, but the basic principle is the same as that of home and corporate routers. That is to say, whether on the Internet or in the home, Corporate Lan, packets are transmitted in the same way, which is a major feature of the Internet.

However, the router used by the operators is different from the small router we use at home. It is a high-speed large router that can connect dozens of network lines. In the backbone of the Internet, there are a large number of these routers, they are connected to each other in a complex way, and network packets are passing through these routers.

In addition, routers differ not only in size but also in the way they connect to each other. Ethernet cables are commonly used in home and corporate LANs, while the Internet uses older telephony and the latest optical communication technologies to transmit network packets in addition to Ethernet connections. The technology used in this section is the most popular part of today's network, can be said to be the crystallization of the most sophisticated technology.

After passing through the backbone network, the network packet finally arrives in the local Area Network where the Web server is located.

Next, it encounters a firewall, which checks the incoming packets. Think of the firewall as the security guard at the door, who checks all the bags that come in to see if any of the dangerous bags are in there. After the check, the network packet may then encounter the cache server. A portion of the web page data is reusable, and this reusable data is stored in the cache server. If the page data you want to access happens to be found in the cache server, you can read the data directly from the cache server without bothering the Web server. In addition, in large Web sites, there may be load balancers that distribute messages across multiple Web servers, and there may be services that distribute content through caching servers distributed across the Internet. After these mechanisms, the network packets arrive at the Web server.

When the network packet arrives at the Web Server, the data is unpacked and restored to the original request message, which is then handed over to the Web server program. Like the client, this is done by the protocol stack (network control software) in the operating system. Next, the Web server program analyzes the meaning of the request message, loads the data into the response message as instructed, and then sends it back to the client.

When the response reaches the client, the browser reads the data from the web page and displays it on the screen. At this point, a series of operations to access the Web server are complete, and our journey of discovery has come to an end.

How the Internet is Connected?

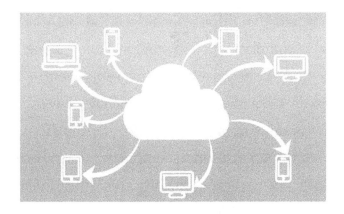

This Network is the Access Network AN (Access Network), which is also known as the local Access Network, or resident Access Network. This is a special kind of computer network. As we explained above, a user must be able to access the Internet through an ISP. Since there are many technologies available for accessing the Internet from a user's home, there are situations where multiple access network technologies can be used to connect to the Internet. The access network itself is neither the core nor the periphery of the Internet. An access network is a network between a client system and the first router (also known as an edge router) on the Internet. From the scope of coverage, many access networks also belong to local area networks. From the point of view of the role, the access network is only to allow users to connect with the Internet "bridge" role. In the early days of the Internet, users used telephone lines to dial into the Internet at very low rates (from a few thousand to a few tens of thousands of bits per second), so the term access network was not used.

Basic Components of Computer Network

No matter which definition can be seen above, the computer network is a complete system composed of some hardware equipment and corresponding software system. The basic components of a computer network include a computer (or a computer terminal with only basic computer functions), network connections and communication equipment, transmission media, and network communication software (including network communication protocols).

These basic computer network components are divided into hardware systems and software systems.

Computer Network Hardware System

Computer Network hardware system refers to the visible physical facilities in the computer network, including all kinds of computer equipment, transmission media, network equipment, these three major parts.

1. Computer Equipment

The purpose of building a computer network is to provide a platform for network communication among users of various computer equipment, such as user access, data transmission, file sharing, remote control and so on. A computer device is a variety of computers (such as pcs, computer servers, computer terminals, laptop computers, IPad and the like) that are controlled and used by network users. The main applications of the network are performed on these computer devices. In fact, now the computer network and the telecommunication network are somewhat overlapped. Many telecommunication terminals can also be connected to the computer network, such as the smartphones we use now Can carry on the data transmission between the USB interface and the computer, even carries on the remote communication.

Note that in the traditional definition of a computer network, a computer network requires at least one fully functional physical computer (others can be terminals). With the rise of Network virtualization technology, the current computer network can be a virtual machine (such as VPC, VMWare, etc.) in a physical computer simulation of a number of independent computer systems, forming a virtual computer network This network can also perform functions that can only be performed in many physical computer networks.

2. Network Equipment

In a computer network system, network equipment usually refers to equipment other than computer equipment Such as network card, bridge, gateway, Modem, switch, router, hardware firewall, hardware IDS (intrusion detection system), hardware IPS (intrusion prevention system) , broadband access server (Bras) , UPS (uninterruptible power supply) , etc. Wlan Network Card, WLAN AP, WLAN Router, WLAN switch, etc.

Network equipment is used to construct the network topology in the "communication subnet", and the communication lines (that is, "transmission medium") together to form the framework of the whole computer network. Of course, the simplest network, in fact, does not need any network equipment, that is, two terminal computers with serial/parallel port cable directly connected to the peer-to-peer network. But this network is not really a computer network, for now, such a computer network does not have much practical significance.

3. Transmission Medium

The transmission medium is simply the network line, is the network communication "road". Without these transmission media, the network communication signal will not know where to transmit, also cannot transmit, just like there is no road ahead, we cannot move forward. Of course, the transmission medium can be physically tangible, such as coaxial cable (which is also used in cable television), twisted pair, optical cable (also known as an optical fiber), etc, or invisible For example, the transmission medium used in various wireless networks is, in fact, electromagnetic waves. Wireless Computer Network (WCN) is to realize the connection of each node in WCN by the electromagnetic wave. Of course, in the coaxial cable, twisted pair, optical cable, and these transmission media.

4. Computer Network Software System

These computer network communication and application software refer to the computer program installed in the terminal computer for computer network communication or application. First of all, there is a network application platform, such as computers and servers installed, with the computer network communication functions of the operating system. Operating Systems for computer network communications are also installed on devices such as switches, routers, and firewalls. For example, Windows, Linux, UNIX, CatOS for Cisco Switch/router/ Firewall, IOS for IOS, and Comware for H3C switch/router/ firewall.

In addition to the operating system, the network communication protocols, such as TCP / IP Protocol Cluster, Ieee 802 protocol cluster, PPP, PPPoE, IPX / SPX, and VLAN, STP, RIP, OSPF, BGP, etc. Finally, it is necessary to carry out a variety of specific network applications tool software, such as our common Qq, MSN instant messaging software, Outlook, Firefox, Sendmail and other email software, for dial-up PPP, PPPoE protocol IPSEC, PPTP, L2TP and so on for VPN communication.

How the Internet is given to people?

Internet Communications

Let's take a closer look at how the actual network is constructed. People generally use Internet access services when they connect to the Internet at home or at work. It is even possible to communicate with the target address through an "edge network" or "backbone".

Mobile Communications

As soon as the phone is turned on, it will automatically communicate wirelessly with the nearest base station. The base station is equipped with a special cell phone base antenna, and the base itself is the "access layer" of the network. When a cell phone terminal sends a signal to another terminal, the request goes all the way to the base station that registers the phone number on the other end. If the other party answers the call, a communication connection is established between the two phones. The communications requests collected by the base station are collected in the Control Center ("Edge Network"), which is then connected to the backbone of the Interconnection Control Center. This mobile network is structured much like an Internet access service.

LTE and Voice Call

His limited data communications. And LTE is regarded as the transition technology from 3G to 4G, which is a kind of mobile communication standard made by 3GPP (the organization that makes the 3rd Generation Mobile Communication Standard made up of standardization bodies in different countries). Depending on the situation, it can achieve up to 300 Mbps down and 75 MBPS UP wireless communications.

In the LTE standard, the use of TCP / IP over the entire network is necessary because the voice is also transmitted as an IP packet. (today, voice communications are also largely digital, using TCP / IP Technology.). However, in reality, it is often impossible to replace all the hardware devices in the network all at once. In this case, the techniques of CSFB (CSFB) can be used. The technology allows voice calls to be transmitted only over cellular networks. Keeps it in line with the original sound process.

Chapter 2.   Wireless hardware and standard

This is not unconnected to the havoc that potential cybercriminals can wreck on a network with lax security measures. In this chapter, I will discuss the concept of wireless technology security extensively in order to assist you to have a deeper understanding of the concept, the potential security threats, and the practical security tips that can serve as preventive measures against these threats.

Types of wireless network security

The increased global concern about the security of wireless networks has triggered the need for different security measures to be developed with the goal of reinforcing the security of wireless networks. Wireless network security can be achieved through some standards and algorithms that are specifically designed for that purpose. Some of these security measures are:

Wi-Fi Protected Access (WPA)

The Wi-Fi Protected Access is a security certification and security program for securing wireless computer networks designed to address some of the weaknesses in the Wired Equivalent Privacy (WEP). When you use WPA encryption for securing your Wi-Fi networks, you need a passphrase, otherwise known as a password, or a network security key. The passphrases are usually made up of numbers and letters. To establish a connection to the Wi-Fi network, the computer and whatever other connected devices must use the passphrase.

If you personally own the Wi-Fi network, it is advisable that you choose your own password when setting up the Wi-Fi network. Your password must be lengthy and be made up of alphanumeric characters and special characters to increase the security level of the password to prevent someone without the right authorization access to your network. When choosing a passphrase, you should also ensure that your passphrase is unique and cannot be easily guessed or cracked.

Wired Equivalent Policy (WEP)

WEP has been around for years. It's one of the security methods that have been around for years, especially for supporting older devices. The WEP security technique is not difficult to implement. You will trigger a network security key whenever you enable the WEP. The security key will encrypt any information that the computer shares with any other computer on the network. WEP was made known to the public by the Institute of Electrical and Electronics Engineers (IEEE) in 1979. This is a not-for-profit organization that has the responsibility of developing the right standards that can be adopted in electronic transmissions. There are two types of WEP. They are:

- Shared key authentication: This is a channel through which a computer can access a WEP-based wireless network. If a computer has a wireless modem, SKA will allow it to have access to the WEP network to enable it to exchange both unencrypted and encrypted data. For this authentication type to function efficiently, a wireless access point must match a WEP encryption key that has been obtained prior to the time of use by the connecting computer.

The connection process starts when the computer contacts the access point with an authentication request. In response to the request, the access point will generate a challenge text, a sequence of characters, for the computer. The computer will use its WEP key for encrypting the challenge text and later transmit it to the access point. After receiving the message, the access point will decrypt it and subsequently compare the result of the decrypted message with the main challenge text. If there are no mistakes in the decrypted message, the access point will immediately send the authentication code needed by the connecting computer to the computer. Then, finally, the connecting computer will accept the sent authentication code and thus is integrated into the network throughout the session or throughout the period when the connecting computer is within the original access point's range.

On the other hand, if there is a discrepancy between the original text and the decrypted message, the access point will prevent the computer from becoming a part of the network.

- Open system authentication: The Open System Authentication (OSA) refers to a technique that allows a computer to gain unrestricted access to a WEP-based wireless network. With this system authentication, any computer that has a wireless modem can gain access to any network where it can receive unencrypted files. For the Open System Authentication to work, the computer's Service Set Identifier (SSID) should be the same with that of the wireless access point. The SSID refers to some well-arranged characters that uniquely assign names to a Wireless Local Area Network. The whole process occurs in just three stages.

First, the computer will send a request to the access point for authentication. When the access point receives the request, it will randomly generate an authentication code that is intended for use at the right time: during the session. Finally, the computer will take the authentication code and thus integrate into the network throughout the duration of the session and as long as the computer is within the range of the access point. You need a Shared Key Authentication (SKA), a better and stronger authentication technique, if you find it necessary to transfer encrypted data between a wireless-equipped computer and the access point of a WEP network.

Top ways to secure your wireless network

Today, the popularity of wireless networks comes at a price: cybercriminals are always on the lookout for possible loopholes they can exploit to breach your security and compromise your data. Hence, it is a matter of urgency to find some ways to beef the security of your wireless network to prevent these criminals from breaching your security. Here are some security measures that can guarantee the security of your wireless network:

Understand the principle behind wireless networks

Understanding the principle behind how a wireless network works can be of help in safeguarding your wireless networks. If you want to go wireless, you need to connect a DSL modem, a cable, or any other access point to a wireless router. The router will then send a signal out through the air to the desired destination, which may sometimes be a couple of hundred feet away. Any device that is connected within the range will be able to pull the signal and have access to the Internet. With this understanding, you are likely more willing to take necessary precautions to ensure that no one has access to your network besides yourself and other authorized people.

Encrypt your wireless network

If you are using a wireless network at home or in your office, make it a point of duty to encrypt any type of information you want to transfer over the network to prevent eavesdroppers from gaining access to your confidential information. When you encrypt a data, it is scrambled into a code that others cannot gain access to. Encrypting your data is obviously the most potent way of shutting out intruders from your network.

There are two encryption techniques for the encryption: WPA and WEP. You should always use the same encryption for your router, computer, and other devices. If you need ideas, give WPA2 a try. This encryption technique is efficient and will secure your network against hackers. If you use wireless routers, they always have their encryption turned off. Turn this feature on to secure your network. You will find how to do this if you go through the router's manual. If you can't find the instruction on the manual, visit the router company's official website for the instruction.

Limit access to your network

It is also your responsibility to ensure that only certain devices are allowed to access your wireless network. All the devices that are able to effectively communicate with a wireless network are automatically assigned a unique MAC (Media Access Control) address. Wireless routers are designed with a mechanism that they use for allowing devices that have specific MAC address to gain access to a network to ensure the security of your network.

However, you should be cautious when using this security option. Some hackers and other cybercriminals have found a way to mimic MAC addresses and can easily infiltrate your network. Therefore, complement this security technique with some other effective network security techniques.

Secure your router

Your router is another device that deserves protection as well so that your wireless network won't be susceptible to cyber-attack via some loopholes in the security of your router. It is the responsibility of your router to direct traffic between the Internet and your local network. Therefore, protecting your router is the first step towards the protection of your entire network. If you leave your router unprotected, strangers may gain access to your network and thus access your personal and confidential information such as your financial information. If they have complete control of your router, you can't predict what they will do with your network.

Change your router's default name

Your router obviously comes with a default name. This name is sometimes called SSID or the service set identifier. This is the name assigned to the router by the manufacturer. To increase the security of your wireless network, it is advisable that you change this default name and give the router a unique and difficult-to-guess name. Also, don't reveal this name to anyone. If you are the only person with access to the default name, it is almost impossible for the router to be subjected to a security breach.

Change the router's default password(s)

Just as the router comes with a default name, it also comes with a default password or a group of passwords. This password gives you the freedom to set up the router as well as operate it. Hackers are familiar with the default passwords and can use the knowledge to hack your router and gain access to your network if you leave the default password(s) unchanged. Make the password change for both the "administrator" and "user."

The rule of thumb stipulates that you use a combination of letters and numbers, known as alphanumeric characters, as well as long and difficult-to-guess passwords. It is advisable that you use a minimum of 12 characters for your password. You may also include lowercase and uppercase letters. The more complex your password, the more difficult it is for hackers to break. If you are unsure about how to change the password, visit the router company's website, and you will be guided through the process.

Don't always log in as administrator

After you have successfully set up your router, don't keep yourself logged in as administrator. Rather, you should log out immediately if you are not using the router. This will reduce the risk of being piggybacked on during your session in order to have access to your login details and take control of your router. That may have a dire consequence on your network.

Turn off "Remote Management" features

The reason for this security measure is pretty obvious. Some routers' manufacturers offer the option to keep the remote management option turned on in order to provide you with technical support when necessary. Sadly, leaving this option turned on is synonymous to making your financial information available to the public. Hackers may capitalize on the feature to gain access to your router and, invariably, your network. On the other hand, when you leave this feature turned off, controlling your network from a remote location is impossible.

Always update your router

In order for your router to work effectively and be secure, the accompanying software must be regularly updated to fix bugs and other issues. Before setting up your router, visit the router's website to see if you can get the updated software that you can download. It is a course of wisdom to register the router with the manufacturer as well as sign up to receive regular updates to ensure that you are kept in the loop whenever there is a new software version.

Secure your computer

Regardless of the security measures you adopt for your router and other devices that are connected to your network, it is imperative that you secure your computer too. For instance, you can use some protections such as antispyware, antivirus, and firewall to fortify the security of your computer. Remember to keep the software up-to-date as well. Some valuable security tips include using a strong password for your computer and using up-to-date antivirus, antispyware, and firewalls. Don't forget to enable 2-factor authentication as well.

Log out of connected apps

If you access your network via an app, don't keep the app open when you are not using the app. Log out immediately and log in again whenever you want to access the network with the app. Why should you go through this process of logging in and out frequently? Remember that you can lose your phone or have it stolen at any time. Keeping the app open allows others to access your network via the stolen or lost phone. To further increase the security of the network through the app, adopt the password tips. Use a strong password that hackers will have a challenging time hacking so the chances of others gaining access to your network through your app are drastically reduced.

Password your phone

While password-protecting your app is a good idea, think about making your phone inaccessible to others as well. Protecting your phone will create the first barrier against unauthorized access to your phone and your network. I have given a list of practical tips for creating strong and difficult-to-hack passwords. Go through the chapter again and implement the tips. The stronger your password, the more difficult it is to hack your phone and access sensitive information that may be used against you or your network.

Reduce the range of your wireless signal

This is another effective security option you should consider. This is applicable to users whose wireless routers have a very high range while the users are using small spaces for operation. If you are in that group, decrease the signal range. There are two ways to do this. You can either change your wireless channel or change your router's mode to 802.11g rather than the conventional 802.11b or 802.11n. Alternatively, you can place the router in some secluded places such as inside a shoe box or under a bed. You can also wrap a foil around its antennas to perfectly restrict its signals' direction.

Stay under the radar

To hide the visibility of your network and stop your wireless network from broadcasting its presence, disable the router's Service Set Identifier (SSID) to make it "invisible." This will prevent strangers beside your business or home from being aware of the network and its name. This will also reduce the number of people who may be interested in gaining access to your network.

Turn off the network when not in use

This is considered by some experts as "the ultimate in wireless security measures." The reason for this assertion is not far-fetched: if you shut your network down, most hackers will certainly be prevented from breaking in. While it may be impractical to keep switching the network off and on frequently, it is still practical to do it occasionally when you won't be using the network for a long time, perhaps when on vacation or when you will be offline for an extended period of time.

Have antimalware installed on connected devices

It is not out of place to take an inventory of the wide variety of devices connected to the network. When you have a full list of the devices, ensure that they all have antimalware installed on each of the devices for maximum protection against external invasion, especially in devices that can support the protection. Listed above are some effective ways you can close the door to your wireless network to the bad guys and thus prevent your network from being compromised. The suggestions here are practical and very easy to implement.

The tips discussed above have been tested and proven reliable over the years. Since precaution is usually better than cure, taking these steps to boost the security of your network is more rewarding and more effective than waiting until disaster strikes before running from pillar to post looking for a solution to the problem, so increase the immunity of your network and give cybercriminals a second thought about making attempts to breach your security. If you don't implement these tips, you are a sitting duck, an easy target for hackers.

Chapter 3. Wireless Technologies

Wireless signals operate pretty much in the same way that ethernet hubs do. They support back and forth communication. These signals operate in the same frequency to receive and transmit data packets, hence such wireless technologies are half-duplex.

A Wireless LAN uses radio frequencies (RF) that are transmitted from an antenna. Considering how far these signals travel at times, they are prone to vulnerability. There are a lot of factors in the immediate environment that might also be responsible for interfering with the quality of network service delivery.

One of the possible ways of improving the network is to increase the transmission power. However, while increasing the transmission power might work, it also creates a new problem, opening up the network to the possibility of distortion. Besides, higher frequencies do not come cheap either.

The wireless specification 802.11 was created to support network freedom. Under this specification, you do not need licensing in most jurisdictions to operate a wireless network. Therefore, all devices that support wireless connection can communicate without necessarily having to force the administrator or user to create a complex wireless network.

Considering that wireless networks transmit data through radio frequencies, in some areas they are regulated by the same laws that monitor the operation of radio frequencies like AM and FM. The Federal Communications Commission (FCC) in the US oversees the use of wireless devices. In support, the Institute of Electrical and Electronics Engineers (IEEE) establishes the standards upon which the frequencies released by the FCC can be used.

For public use, the FCC allows 900 MHz, 2.4GHz and 5GHz. The first two are identified as the Industrial, Scientific and Medical bands (ISM) while the 5GHz band is Unlicensed National Information Infrastructure band (UNII).

Before you run a wireless network outside of these three bands, therefore, you must seek approval from the FCC. The 802.11b/g wireless network is one of the most commonly used all over the world today.

802.11

This network was the pioneer of WLAN, standardized at 1Mbps and 2Mbps. 802.11 is operated in the 2.4 GHz frequency. While it is popular, it was not until 802.11b was released that its uptake increased. There are many committees in the 802.11 standard, each of which serves a unique purpose.

Components of a wireless network

Wireless networks require fewer components compared to wired networks. Basically, all you need for your wireless network to operate effectively is a wireless NIC and an access point (AP). Once you understand how these two components work, you can install them easily and operate the network without any challenges.

Wireless Network Interface Card (NIC)

Each host must have a wireless network interface to connect to a wireless network. The role of a wireless network interface card is no different from that of a normal network interface card.

Access Point (AP)

You need a central component in the network to enable communication. For a wired network, this would be a switch or a hub. For a wireless network, you need a wireless access point. Most APs have at least two antennas to boost their communication range. They also have a port through which they connect to a wired network.

A wireless network must have some cable running through it. Most wireless networks are connected to a wired network through an AP. The AP bridges the two network types.

Wireless antenna

An antenna in a wireless network serves two roles. It can act as a receiver and a transmitter. At the moment there are two types of antennas you will come across in the market, a directional antenna or an omnidirectional antenna.

While directional antennas are point-to-point, omnidirectional antennas are point-to-multipoint. The directional antennas offer a wider range compared to the omnidirectional antennas in the same gain range. The reason for this is because all the power in a directional antenna is focused to one direction.

Perhaps the challenge of using a directional antenna is that you must be very accurate when positioning its communication points. For this reason, directional antennas are an ideal choice when setting up point-to-point connections, or bridging different access points.

Omnidirectional antennas are popular with APs because more often, clients want to access the network in different directions at any given time. A directional antenna would make this quite a challenge, because the client would have to position their access in one direction to enjoy access.

Setting up a wireless network

You can set up a wireless network in one of two ways. You can either use an ad hoc set up, or infrastructure mode.

Ad hoc setup

For this setup, the devices connected can communicate with one another without having to use an AP. This is what happens when you create an ad hoc wireless network on your laptop to communicate with other devices that can connect to it.

As long as you use the right settings, devices that are connected to the network can share files without any issues. When installing the network, one of the prompts will require you to choose whether you are using an ad hoc mode or infrastructure mode.

For this set up to work, make sure that your computers are within 90 meters of one another. Once they can detect one another, you can communicate and share files. The problem with an ad hot network is that it never scales well, and for this reason you should never use this in an organizational set up. This network is also prone to a lot of collisions. One of the reasons why ad hoc networks are no longer appealing today is because the cost of obtaining APs is very affordable, it does not make sense to run an ad hoc network.

Infrastructure mode

Infrastructure mode allows you to connect to a network, enjoying the benefits of a wired network without the unsightly cables. In this mode, the NIC communicates through an AP instead of directly to whichever device is on the network as is the case in an ad hoc setting.

All forms of communication between host devices on this network must pass through the AP. When connected to this network, all the hosts appear to the other devices on the network in the same way they appear on a wired network. Before you connect your client to on this mode, make sure you understand some of the basic concepts, especially security.

Factors to consider when installing a large wireless network

When connecting a large wireless network, you must adhere to specific design considerations. A lot of organizations today use mesh infrastructure. One of the reasons for this is because it is decentralized and dependable. Mesh infrastructure is also one of the most affordable setups, so most organizations find it feasible. These networks are affordable because each host only needs to broadcast data packets as far as the nearest host.

In such a network, each host in the network is a repeater, so instead of one host struggling to transmit the data all over the network, it carries it to the next host who then passes it on and so forth until the data is transmitted to the intended recipient. A mesh interface, therefore, is a reasonable consideration especially when you are building a network over a difficult topography.

Mesh topology is implemented with several fail-safes in the form of redundancy connections between hosts. Since the design basically is built around making sure redundancies are a thing of the past, a mesh topology is perfect for a large institution or installation.

Mesh networks are highly reliable. Considering that each host on the network is connected to many other hosts, any one of these hosts dropping out of the network does not affect the system. Perhaps one of the hosts malfunctions or experiences a software challenge. Instead of data hanging, the other hosts on the network simply find an alternative route and continue transmitting the data packets. Anyone on the network will barely notice one of the hosts is missing.

Would you employ a mesh network on a home network? It sounds so good in theory, but in application, a mesh network is not ideal for a home network, or for any small organization that operates on a very tight budget.

Signal degradation

Whenever you are installing a wireless network, one of the things you have to worry about is signal degradation. All 802.11 networks use radio frequencies. With this in mind, the strength of the signal will be determined by and affected by a lot of factors, most of which you have no control over. A weak network is quite an unreliable network, and anyone who connects to it would be frustrated. The following are some of the reasons why you might have fluctuating wireless network signals:

• Interference

Interference from outside will affect your network. Given this consideration, there are so many sources that might cause interference as long as they exist within this range.

Some of the causes of interference are in your vicinity, and include another wireless network, mobile phones, microwave appliances, and Bluetooth devices. Any device that uses a transmission frequency close to the frequency your 802.11 wireless network uses will interfere with the network.

- Wireless network protocols

Which protocol did you use when installing the wireless network? We already know there are different protocols that exist under 802.11. Each of the protocols operate under a specific maximum frequency range. For example, an 802.11b protocol will conflict with an 802.11g protocol.

- Barriers

Wherever you have a wireless network, always remember that barriers can affect the ability to transmit data on it. The signal will be weaker if it has to bypass a number of walls to get to the user. A wireless network with a range of around 100 feet might have the range drop to around 20 feet if there are so many walls within the office block. The thickness of the walls also impedes network access.

- Distance

This one is pretty obvious. The further away you are from the wireless network, the weaker your signal will be. Most access points today are built with a range of 100 meters. To extend this range, you must use amplifiers.

Chapter 4.   Managing Routers and Switches

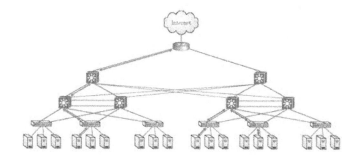

Remote Administration

It's not always possible to use a console cable to perform changes to Cisco device configurations. What if the Router is at a remote site, or you are working from home? Luckily Cisco allows remote administration using two technologies, Telnet and SSH.

SSH is the preferred method of remote administration because it encrypts data in transit, while telnet does not. By default SSH Version 1 is activated but SSH Version 2 can be enabled manually for increased security.

Telnet

To enable telnet access, you must modify the configuration of the virtual terminal (vty) lines using the line command in global configuration mode.

You must specify the virtual terminal lines you would like to modify, in this case we are modifying the first 5 lines, 0-4. That means a total of 5 remote connections can be ongoing at once. Different hardware models can support more than just 5 vty's.

When you are configuring the vty lines, you will notice the prompt has changed to (config-line)# to illustrate you are in the line configuration submode.

Next, specify a telnet password using the (config-line)#password command.

By default, the vty lines are disabled. To allow users to connect, the (config-line)#login command must be used.

(config)#line vty 0 4

(config-line)#password example

(config-line)#login

SSH

To enable logins using the more secure SSH, you must first enable AAA (Authentication, Authorization, and Accounting) and generate an RSA key used for the cryptographic functions of SSH.

To enable AAA globally, execute the (config)#aaa new-model command from global configuration mode.

Next, we must generate an RSA key. A domain name is required to generate an RSA key, and can be specified using the (config)#ip domain name x command.

Next, enable SSH Version 2 globally with the following command (config)#ip ssh version 2.

We need to create a user to login via SSH using the username command. Simply type (config)#username x secret x. Remember, always use secret passwords over unencrypted passwords!

Lastly we must modify the VTY lines to only accept logins via SSH. Enter the vty line configuration using the line command as in the Telnet example. Then specify the login type using (config-line)# transport input ssh.

Example:

(config)#aaa new-model

(config)#ip domain name example.com

(config)#crypto key generate rsa modulus 2048

(config)#ip ssh version 2

(config)#username x secret x

(config)# line vty 0 4

(config-line)# transport input ssh

Enabling SCP for secure file copy

There are many occasions when an administrator will need to copy a file to or from a remote Cisco device. When the device is physically present, copying files using a USB flash drive is simple and painless, but that opinion is not always available.

Methods to do so include FTP, TFTP, HTTP, and SCP. However, all but the last method are unencrypted, meaning anyone could spy in on the data being transferred.

To enable the SCP server and to allow encrypted file transfer via the SSH protocol, use the following commands. First you must enable Authentication, Authorization, and Accounting (AAA) globally and create the username and password to be used. Users must be authorized to execute commands (such as scp), and must be given a privilege level of 15 to allow files to be copied. Finally, the SCP server can be enabled.

TIP

It is important to weigh the advantage of this functionality vs its security concerns. Of course you can always just change the privilege level to 15 only when you are SCPing a file, and then change it right back.

(config)#aaa new-model

(config)#aaa authentication login default local

(config)#aaa authorization exec default local none

(config)#username root secret xxxxxx

(config)#username root privilege 15

(config)#ip scp server enable

If you are using Windows, use a SCP client such as Filezilla or WinSCP to copy files to the Cisco device.

To copy a file from a Linux or OSX computer to a Cisco device using SCP, use the scp command as shown below.

$scp ./c1900-universalk9-mz.SPA.151-4.M7.bin
root@69.163.56.156:c1900-universalk9-mz.SPA.151-4.M7.bin

This command copies an image file from the local directory on the computer to the root directory of the flash: file system on the remote Cisco device. The username configured on the Cisco device is root, illustrated by root@.

Managing Configurations

Backing Up Configuration Files

Backing up configuration files is a simple process in IOS. Every time you use the

#copy running-config startup-config command you are writing the configuration to flash memory, NVRAM. If you would like to backup the configuration file elsewhere, simply save the file to another location, such as a USB drive or SCP server.

For example, to backup the configuration to a USB drive, first find the name of the usb drive using the #show file systems command. In this example, the name of the usb drive is usbflash0.

Next, copy to running config to a filename of your choice on the device.

#copy running-config usbflash0:backup.txt

You can also copy your configuration to a SCP Server using the syntax below.

#copy running-config scp://192.168.1.1/

TIP

Some settings are not backed up in configuration files. For example the generation of SSH keys. These types of commands must be added to configuration files manually, or else they must be rerun when the configuration is restored.

Restoring Configuration Files

It is a good idea to write your device configurations on your computer rather than configuring the routers and switches by hand. This allows you to create simple templates that can be modified for the occasion and allows for easy version control and backup through services such as git. If you are unfamiliar with version control, a great place to start learning git is at https://github.com/.

Git allows for a centrally managed, version controlled, secure location for your configuration files. These configs can then be redeployed or adapted at a moment's notice on any failed hardware or new site needs.

A configuration file is simply a list of commands run on the device sequentially. Think of it as a faster way to copy and paste into the terminal window.

To create a configuration file, simply write the commands as you would type them You can see some examples in the appendix section of this book. Test configurations out on lab equipment to create a template you can use for future devices.

To load the configuration file onto the router, copy the configuration file from USB or SCP into the device's running config using the copy command. For example:

#copy usbflash1:config.txt running-config

or

#copy scp://192.168.1.10/config.txt running-config

TIP

Cisco configurations are additive - meaning copying a configuration over an existing one may cause conflicts. Its best to reset a router to factory defaults before copying over a new configuration file, to make certain there are no conflicts. We'll go over this process later in this section.

Archive Feature

It is very important to back up configuration files for Cisco devices. This creates a record of what changes have been made and gives a reference to roll back to.

To automatically back up configuration changes to a remote host, use the Archive feature on Cisco IOS. I would recommend using SCP for this procedure to keep your configuration data encrypted in transit. The example below copies the timestamped configuration to the home directory of bob.

(config)#archive

(config-archive)#path scp://bob@172.16.1.10/~

To archive the current configuration, execute the following command in privileged exec mode:

#archive config

You can also force archiving configurations upon executing the copy running-config startup-config or write memory commands with the configuration below:

(config-archive)#write-memory

To check out the recent archives, use the show archive command:

#show archive

And you can rollback to a previous configuration as well using the configure replace command.

#configure replace scp://172.16.1.10/-Jul--3-17-59-36.018-0

Factory Defaults

From the Command Line

If you have privileged exec (enable) access to the router or switch, the easiest way to reset the device to factory default is using the #write erase command.

This command will clear all configuration settings from NVRAM (the startup-config), and upon rebooting the system will return to factory defaults. After clearing the NVRAM, you must reboot the device with the #reset command so the machine can restart with the default configuration. Do not save the running config to NVRAM when prompted, or you will have to restart the process after a lengthy reboot!

Resetting Switches

If you do not have privileged exec access to the device, (you have forgotten the password, for example) there are still options! Most switches can be reset by holding the Reset button, or in some cases the Mode button. To Reset 3650 Switches for example, press the mode button (pictured below) for 10 seconds.

One minor caveat of Cisco switches is that VLAN data (show vlan) persists after a reset to factory defaults. Why? Because the VLAN information is stored in a separate file in flash memory. If you want to reset the VLAN information as well, you must delete the vlan.dat file in the flash filesystem.

To clear VLAN information, delete the vlan configuration file on flash. The effect will take place after a reboot.

#delete flash:/vlan.dat

Resetting Routers

Most routers do not have reset buttons. Instead, you can instruct the system to boot factory defaults by changing the configuration register.

The configuration register is responsible for many configuration options on Cisco equipment. It is not often directly configured, as it is capable of manipulating the startup sequence. In this case, that is exactly what we want to do! We can instruct the system to skip loading the startup configuration file stored in flash, loading the default configuration instead.

Modifying the control register can take place from ROM Monitor mode. This is an very basic environment similar to the BIOS on a PC.

To enter ROM Monitor mode press the break key (which is not on all keyboards) from a terminal during device start up.

TIP

If you do not have a break key, putty allows you to enter ROM Monitor mode by right clicking on the window and selecting Special Command > Break. In Minicom, the break key is 'Ctrl-A' and then 'F'.

The below commands instruct the system to load a default configuration.

ROM Monitor Example:

rommon 1 > confreg 0x2142

rommon 2 > reset

Now you are back into the device! Clear the old configuration with the #write erase command and you should be back in business.

Don't forget to change the config register back to default again, so it will subsequently load configuration files from NVRAM. You can do that in IOS using the (config)#config-register command.

(config)# config-register 0x2102

Upgrading Cisco IOS

It is best to have all of your Cisco equipment running the same version of Cisco IOS. This allow you to have a consistent environment with a minimum of conflicts due to incompatible versions and makes it easier to troubleshoot/find any issues caused by IOS bugs.

To upgrade your devices you must first download the IOS image you would like to use from Cisco's website. Login and search for your device under Support > Downloads. Once you have found your model, choose Software on Chassis > IOS Software.

Often Cisco will show you the recommended or suggested images for your switch or router. This is a good place to start and you can look over the release notes for each image to determine if it will work well in your environment. Once you have chosen your image, download it to proceed.

Once you have the image there are multiple ways to copy it over to your system such as USB, FTP, TFTP, SCP, and HTTP.

If you have physical access to a device with a USB port, the simplest method is to copy it over is from a USB stick which is formatted with the FAT32 file system. Simply copy your IOS image onto the flash drive and plug it into the USB port of the router or switch.

When you plug the USB stick into the router or switch, it will show up as device usb0: or usbflash0: or similar. You can check the path to your USB stick using the #show file systems command. In the example below, the usb stick shows up as usbflash0:

Once the USB stick is inserted, simply copy the IOS image from the flash drive to the local flash memory on the router or switch. You can use the copy command to do so.

For example:

#copy usbflash0:c1841-ipbasek9-mz.151-4.M.bin flash:

This command will copy the image stored on the usb drive to the onboard flash memory of the router.

You can also experiment with copying from other sources, such as FTP, TFTP, HTTP, HTTPS, and SCP servers.

Many administrators choose to use TFTP to transfer images and configuration files because of its easy setup. But remember - TFTP is unencrypted and should not be used over the public internet!

To transfer files via TFTP, use the copy command specifying TFTP as the source. You will be prompted for the TFTP server address, source (remote) filename, and destination (local) filename.

For Example:

(config)#copy tftp flash

Once the copy is complete, you can choose the IOS image to load on next boot using the boot system command. It's a good idea to issue the no boot system command first, to clear the current boot settings.

These commands instruct the system to load the specified IOS image on next reboot.

(config)#no boot system

(config)#boot system flash:1841-ipbasek9-mz.151-4.M.bin

TIP

The boot setting is stored in the configuration file. If you clear the configuration Cisco devices default to boot IOS images in alphabetical order - that usually means the oldest image first, assuming you have not changed the name of the images.

Because of this, you may prefer to delete the older image from flash, keeping only the newer image. Only do this once you have verified everything is working as expected!

Chapter 5.   Advanced Configurations

Dynamic Host Configuration Protocol (DHCP)

DHCP is used by client computers to automatically receive an IP address on the network. Multiple DHCP servers are available, such as Microsoft DHCP Server on Windows, or dhcpd on Linux. Cisco also provides a DHCP server in IOS which is fairly straightforward to configure, and does not require the configuration/maintenance of any external DHCP server.

The DHCP server is configured per subnet and requires a physical or Vlan interface to be present on the subnet to function.

Basic DHCP Configuration

To configure the DHCP server, you must specify a DHCP pool name, the network address, a default search domain to be given to clients, a DNS server, and a default gateway. All this is done in the DHCP configuration mode. See the simple example below:

(config)# ip dhcp pool mypool

(dhcp-config)# network 192.168.1.0

(dhcp-config)# domain-name mydomain.com

(dhcp-config)# dns-server 8.8.8.8 8.8.4.4

(dhcp-config)# default-router 192.168.1.1

TIP

The cisco device has to have an interface on the configured network, in this case the 192.168.1.0 network, to assign DHCP leases in the pool. For example, hosts connected to gi0/0 configured with ip 192.168.1.1 will receive addresses from the pool above.

DHCP Options

DHCP options pass optional configuration information onto clients. Example uses of DHCP options include specifying a PXE boot server, time server, or log server to be used by the client. There are a large number of DHCP options which can be configured, which ones you require, if any, depends strongly on your environment.

DHCP Options can be configured using the (dhcp-config)#option option_number command inside of the corresponding DHCP pool. The example below configures a PXE boot server and image name.

(dhcp-config)# option 66 ip 10.0.0.2

(dhcp-config)# option 67 ascii pxelinux.0

DHCP Reservations

To reserve certain addresses for static assignment use the excluded-address command in global configuration mode.

(config)# ip dhcp excluded-address 192.168.1.1 192.168.1.100

The above command prevents the DHCP server from assigning addresses 192.168.1.1-192.168.1.100 to clients.

Chapter 6. IPv6 vs IPv4

There are many activities taking place today to move further both the development and implementation of IPv6 addressing technology. Although, IPv6 is becoming more and more a convincing technology, yet it prefers the role of a spectator rather than that of an actor in the big arena of the Internet. In the following sections let's unveil the IPv6 addressing technology, always compared with the existing technology with that of IPv4 addressing technology.

Once upon the time...

Decades ago, it all began as a need for data communication, or rather as a need for "sharing" the resources between computers. Years later, in 1974 Vinton G. Cerf and Robert E. Kahn through a research paper proposed the primary protocols to be used for the communication on the ARPANET. Always according to them, this set of protocols would be called TCP/IP and will consist of TCP protocol (operating in transport layer of the OSI model) and IP protocol (operating in network layer of the OSI model). That led to a birth of the Internet protocol TCP/IP, the initial specification of which will pass through four versions to reach the climax with the fourth version IPv4 in 1979. Nearly a decade from the time it appeared, the fourth version of the TCP/IP was standardized through the ARPANET's Request for Comments (RFC) documents.

Back to the future...

The beginning of the 21st century revealed numerous problems in the field of data communication. Whilst the demands for an Internet connection from among individuals and businesses were increasing, alongside with that the lack of the available IPv4 addresses were increasing too. Forecasts of experts went as far as claiming that in the near future there will be no available IPv4 addresses. All this escalated the need for action in the field of development of new technologies for communication based on IP addresses. Numerous ideas produced numerous proposals which brought only one solution that of IPv6 addressing technology. Thus, in 1993 by several Internet groups like CNAT, Nimrod, and others the IPv6 addressing technology was proposed as a new set of communication protocols. In 1995, the base specification has been compiled. Also, in this year, the working group of IPv6 began the WIDE project to move further development of the IPv6 environment. The IPv6 addressing technology is often known as IPng meaning the IP next generation.

IPv4 vs IPv6

The following table compares the IPv4 features with that of IPv6:

IPv4	IPv6
32 bits or 4 Bytes IP address	128 bits or 16 Bytes IP address
2^{32} available IP addresses	2^{128} available IP addresses
decimal representation of IP address	hexadecimal representation of IP address
somehow easy to remember IP addresses	hardly to remember IP addresses
IP address types available: unicast, multicast, and broadcast	IP address types available: unicast, multicast, and anycast
it needs and uses NAT	it does needs and does not uses NAT
configuration is mainly manual	it employs the auto configuration

it uses IPsec for security	IPsec is a key security technology
solid QoS	enhanced QoS
complicated routing	advanced routing

IPv6 advantages compared to IPv4

The expansion of the IP addresses space is not the only feature that IPv6 addressing technology provides to the Internet and your LAN or WAN. Additionally, IPv6 offers the following:

· the simple format of the IP datagram head, which enables the implementation of faster routing techniques in hardware level,

· supports the new extensions in the IP datagram head, including the possibilities of inclusion of additional heads that can be created in the future,

· replacement of certain remaining options in IPv4 specification, enabling sufficient space for expansion of additional options that may be needed in the future,

· ability to determine which datagrams require special treatment when it comes to controlling the flow. This will enable the real-time handling of IP datagrams queues (required for real-time voice and video communications in IP-based networks) that usually in IPv4 is powered by other protocols.,

- authentication and encryption capabilities to enable secure connections, etc.

Nowadays, the information accessed on the Internet is provided through IPv4-based infrastructure. Despite shortcomings like the lack of public IP addresses or in regard to security, IPv4 continues to serve users across the globe. In that regard, with all exceptional investments made for the development of IPv6, the following remains to be clarified:

- because of shortcomings in the implementation of IPv6, probably other techniques will be developed that will keep "alive" IPv4?

- either the future of IPv6 will indeed be bright, or it will be concluded as a "great extraordinary experiment" providing an excellent platform for the development of a future to come addressing technologies such that of "IPv8"?

Despite the forecasts or conclusions, time will tell whether the IPv6 addressing technology will remain a choice and the right solution for the next generation of computer networks!

Chapter 7.   The Internet's big arena

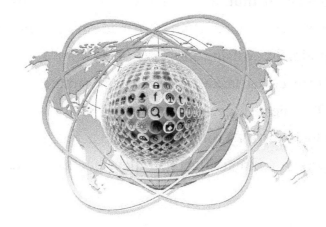

"The Internet is becoming the town square for the global village of tomorrow." Bill Gates

Some call it the network of networks, and some call it the biggest computer network in the world. Nevertheless, it is the Internet like spider net that has covered the globe and has touched every sphere of life of individuals and businesses. On the following sections, you will learn about the past of the Internet, and the most commonly used services on the Internet.

Once upon the time...

No one can explain the history of the Internet better than the Internet itself! Everything started with the US government's project to build a stable and tolerant-in-defects communication network through a computer network. Thus, in the '60s DARPA became the first research project of the US Department of Defense that would deal with research and development of the communication networks. The involvement of research centers and academic institutions in DARPA project along with the development achievements that were made at that time, made this project gradually evolving into ARPANET and MILNET. While MILNET project was tasked to support operational requirements, ARPANET project undertook to support the need for research (InternetSociety.org). From 1962 to 1985, the Internet already built his profile summarizing the achievements of his character as follows:

· the implementation of the first WAN that connected SRI, the University of Utah, UC Santa Barbara and UCLA,

· determining an open architecture technology driven by transfers of packets,

· determining the TCP/IP protocol suite for communication,

· determining the IP addresses in 32-bit format,

· implementation of the e-mail service,

· standardization of record keeping documents called Request for Comments (RFC),

· determining the protocols such as DNS, IGP, EGP, and other FTP,

· the establishment of bodies such as IETF dealing with protocols standardization and ICANN dealing with the maintenance of interaction between domain names, IP addresses, port numbers for applications and other parameters,

· global reach in seven continents,

· as well as many other achievements.

Internet services

No doubt, the Internet is filled with a wide variety of services both in content as well as in functionality. This section lists some of the most well-known services of the Internet in the past and today.

· telnet – remote access service

· File Transfer Protocol (FTP) – file sharing service on the Internet

· e-Mail – service for sending and receiving electronic mail

· UseNet – the service of posted conversations and file sharing

· Internet Relay Chat (IRC) – service of real time conversations

· Hypertext Markup Language (HTML) – programming language for developing web pages and web sites

· World Wide Web (WWW) – service of interconnected system of hypertext documents

· blog – a web site that contains an electronic diary

- e-Commerce – service for selling and buying through the Internet

  - social network – service for bringing people together

The history of mankind recognizes no other technology that achieved more than the Internet. While the past of the Internet seems to be quite dynamic and with dedication, its future looks equally as challenging and intriguing. Projects like Internet2, Internet of Things, Internet of Everything, etc., are just few of the efforts that are being made to advance existing Internet. Regardless, the Internet continues to be a massive platform of information and communication technology.

Chapter 8.   Subnetting Basics

Subnetting is the process used to divide a physical network into smaller logical subnetworks or subnets, which were designed to solve the shortage problem of IP addresses on the Internet. In an IP address, there is a host segment and a network segment.

Subnetting allows companies and organizations to add subnetworks without having to get another network number through their Internet Service Providers (ISPs). It also allows them to reduce their network traffic as well as conceal their network complexity. It is necessary when a certain network number needs to be allocated over several segments in a Local Area Network (LAN).

The Subnet Mask

In order for subnetting to work, the router has to know which part of the host ID needs to be used for the subnet network ID. This can be done by using the subnet mask, which is a 32-bit number. This subnet mask is used to differentiate the network components of IP addresses by dividing them into network addresses and host addresses. It does this by using bit of arithmetic.

When the subnet mask bit multiples the network address, the underlying subnetwork is revealed. Just like IP addresses, subnet masks are written using the dotted decimal notation.

A subnet mask is used to design the subnets or subnetworks that connect to the local networks. It identifies the size and the number of subnets. In this case, the size refers to the number of hosts being addressed.

You can make a subnet mask by getting the 32-bit value of your IP address. Decide on how many subnets you wish to make. Conversely, you may think of how many nodes are necessary for every subnet. Then, you have to set the subsequent network bits to 1. You also have to set the host bits to 0. Whatever 32-bit value you get, that is your subnet mask.

In addition, the subnet mask pinpoints the endpoints of the IP addresses for the subnet. It is called a subnet mask because it masks out the host bits so that only the network ID that starts the subnet is left. Once you find out the start and the size of the subnet, you will be able to determine its end with ease. The end of the subnet is the broadcast ID.

For instance, two host addresses are reserved for specific purposes in a network. The 255 address becomes the broadcast address.

When this is done, it cannot be given to the host. The 0 address becomes the network identification or the network address.

Subnetting Calculations

IP address bits representing the network ID are generally represented by 1 while IP address bits representing the host ID are generally represented by 0. This causes the subnet mask to always have a consecutive string of 1's that is followed by a string of 0's at its left side.

For instance, the subnet mask for a particular subnet, with a network ID consisting of a 16-bit network and a 4-bit subnet ID, is

As you can see, the first twenty bits are all 1's while the rest of the bits are 0's. So, you can say that the complete network ID has 20 bits while the real host ID part of the subnetted address only has 12 bits.

In order for you to be able to identify the IP address' network ID, your router should have both a subnet mask and an IP address. It should be able to perform a bitwise operation known as logical AND on your IP address. This process is necessary for extracting its network ID.

In order for you to be able to perform the logical AND, you have to compare every bit in your IP address with its corresponding bit in your subnet mask. In case both of the bits are 1, your resulting network ID bit will also be 1. However, if one of them is 0, your resulting network ID will also be 0.

To help you understand this further, you should take a look at the following example. In this example, you will see how a network address gets extracted from the IP address with a 20-bit subnet mask.

Using the table shown above, your network ID is 144.28.16.0.

Usually, the subnet mask is represented in a dotted decimal notation. Still using the example given above, your resulting 20-bit subnet mask is represented as follows: 255.255.240.0.

You should not mistake your IP address for your subnet mask. The two elements are not the same. The subnet mask does not represent a network or device on the Internet. It is merely a way to indicate the part of the IP address that needs to be used for determining the network ID.

It is actually very easy to tell a subnet mask apart from an IP address. Your cue here is that the first subnet mask octet is 255 at all times. This number is never a valid one for an IP address.

Every IP address has a subnet mask. Each class type, particularly Class A, Class B, and Class C, has a subnet mask called the default subnet mask. The subnet mask is meant to determine which number and type of IP address is necessary for a particular local network. The router or firewall is referred to as the default gateway, and the default subnet mask is represented by the following:

Class A	255.0.0.0
Class B	255.255.0.0
Class C	255.255.255.0

As an administrator, subnetting allows you to divide any single class network number into small parts. The subnets may be subnetted once more into more subnets.

The Benefits of Dividing a Network Into Subnets

When you divide a network into several subnets, you benefit from the following:

The volumes of broadcasts are reduced, which in turn reduce the traffic in the network.

It helps you surpass constraints of the permitted hosts in a LAN.

Users no longer have to open an entire network just to be able to access a work network from home.

Subnetting Steps

Subnetting involves three steps, and these are the following:

1. Identify the number of host bits necessary for subnetting.

How many host bits you used to perform subnetting determines how many hosts and subnets there are for every subnet. So, before you decide on how many host bits you are going to use, you must have an idea of how many hosts and subnets you are going to possibly have later on. A good rule of thumb is to use more bits for your subnet mask than necessary. This helps you save more time when you reassign IP addresses later on.

Anyway, the more host bits you use, the more subnets you can have. However, this also reduces your number of hosts. On the other hand, if you use too few hosts, you will have more hosts but fewer subnets.

2. Identify the new subnetted network IDs.

Depending on how many host bits you used for subnetting, you have to list down your new subnetted network ID's. You can do this through the following ways:

Decimal. You can add a computed increment value to every successive subnetted network ID. Then, you can convert it into dotted decimal notation.

Binary. You can list down all the possible host bit combinations for subnetting. Then, you can convert these combinations into dotted decimal notation.

Whichever method you use, you will get the same result, which is a list of subnetted network ID's.

3. Identify the IP address of each one of the new subnetted network ID's.

Depending on the subnetted network ID's you have, you have to list down all the valid IP addresses used for subnetted network ID's. However, instead of listing these IP addresses one by one, you can identify and enumerate the IP address necessary for every subnetted network ID. You have to define the range of the IP addresses for every subnetted network ID. You can do this through the following ways:

Decimal. You can add values in an incremental manner. Make sure that they correspond to the first and the last IP addresses for the subnetted network IDs. Then, you can convert them into dotted decimal notation.

Binary. You can list down the first and the last IP addresses for the subnetted network ID's. Then, you can convert them into dotted decimal notation.

Whichever method you use, you will get the same result, which is a list of subnetted network ID's.

Configuring IP Addresses

Now that you have learned all about networking and IP subnetting, it is time to put what you have learned into practice. IP configuration is actually quite easy. In this chapter, you will learn how to configure IP addresses to computers and routers using a Packet Tracer.

The Packet Tracer is a visual simulation program created by Cisco Systems. It lets users design network topologies for the purpose of imitating actual computer networks. Through the software, users are able to simulate switch and router configurations via simulated command line interfaces. The Packet Tracer has a drag and drop interface. You can add and delete simulated devices.

Anyway, in order for you to be able to configure IP addresses, you have to create a topology first, such as this one:

Here is a closer look:

In this example, you can see that the copper cross-over cable is used. Keep in mind that this type of cable is used to connect the following: two hubs, two computers, two router interfaces, a hub to a switch, and a cable modem to a router.

You have to be careful when choosing the connection type for your network. You should use the copper straight-through cable when you connect the following: a hub to a server, a switch to a server, a router to a switch, a computer to a hub, and a computer to a switch.

As you can see in the topology shown above, the IP address of Wendy's Laptop is set to 10.0.0.10 while its default gateway is set to 10.0.0.1. PC0, on the other hand, has an IP address of 20.0.0.10 and a default gateway of 20.0.0.1.

You can say that this is a private network based on their IPs and use of router.

Anyway, you have to click on Laptop-PT (Wendy's Laptop) and assign the necessary values for the gateway.

Next, you have to click on the FastEtherneto, which can be seen on the left side of the screen. Once you are there, you have to set the IP address and the subnet mask, such as the following. The Subnet Mask, the MAC address, and the Link Local Address will automatically show up, so you do not have to worry about them.

When you are done, close the window and do the same process with the PC-PT (PCo).

Then, you should click on the router, which in this setup is Router-PT (Routero). Click on the Command Line Interface (CLI). Once you do that, you will see the following:

You will be prompted to answer with a yes or a no. Type in 'no' or 'n' and press the Enter button. Once you do that, you will see the following:

If you see the same thing on your screen, you have now reached the user mode. To get started, you should enable it by typing in 'enable' or simply 'ena'. You will be in the Privileged Mode. Next, you have to type in 'configure terminal' or simply 'config t' or 'conf t'. Press the Enter button and you will reach the Global Configuration Mode.

You are now ready to configure the router interface with the IP address and the subnet mask. When you are done, you should type in 'no shutdown' or simply 'no shut' or 'no sh' to make the interface and line protocol 'up'.

You do not have to type in the entire words if you want to save time. For instance, you can use 'int fo/o' or 'intfao/o' in place of 'interface fastEthernet o/o' and 'ip ad' instead of 'ip address'. Just imagine how much time you will save if you use shortcuts.

Once you see that the Interface Line protocol on FastEthernet0/0 has changed to 'up', you should press the Enter button and then type in 'exit' or simply 'ex'.

Close the window. You will then see that the lights on the ports have turned from Red to Green.

This means that there is already a connection between Router0 and Wendy's Laptop. The lights on the ports between Router0 and PC0 are still Red, though. This is because PC0 has not yet been configured.

To configure PC0, you should do the same thing as you did with Wendy's Laptop.

Do not worry if you make a mistake while typing the commands. You just have to press the Enter button to type the correct one. In the example shown above, 'ip ad 20.0.0.10' was an incomplete command. So, you cannot advance to the next line. You will be given a notification in case you did not type in the correct command. Until you type in the correct one, you will not be able to go to the next line.

You should be able to see that the Interface Line protocol on FastEthernet1/0 has also changed to 'up'. Afterwards, you should press the Enter button and then type in 'exit' or simply 'ex'.

When you are done, you should see that all the lights on the ports have turned to Green:

In order to test the connection, you should 'ping' them using the Simple PDU (P) button, which is located at the right side of the screen. It is the small yellow envelope that is encircled in this photo:

Select it and move it towards Wendy's Laptop. Then, click on Wendy's Laptop and Router0 simultaneously. You will see that it is 'successful'.

You can also move it towards Router0. Click on it and then click on Wendy's Laptop. You will see that it is also 'successful'.

Another way to test the connectivity is to click on Wendy's Laptop and choose Desktop. You will then see the following:

Select Command Prompt from the choices. You will then see a black screen. Type in 'ping 10.0.0.10' and press the Enter button. You will see the following:

This shows that there is a successful connectivity.

Now, you want to test the connectivity between the two computers. In this setup, you have Wendy's Laptop and PC0.

Still using the Simple PDU (P) button, you should ping Wendy's Laptop and PC0. You should see that it is successful.

You can also ping it from PC0 to Wendy's Laptop. Either way, you would get a successful result.

If you want to use the command prompt to check the connectivity between the two end devices or computers, you should ping 20.0.0.10.

If this is the result that you got, then you have a successful connection. It means that the two end devices are able to communicate with each other.

Real-Life Application: You now have a working network! How can you relate this with the real world? Well, you can have a small network that consists of two computers that are connected to the Internet and a router that is connected to a telecommunications company.

Chapter 9.   Subnetting Examples

How to determine a subnet address?

Suppose, you have an IP address 172.16.10.5 and a subnet mask 255.255.255.128(/25). You have to find out the subnet ID of your IP and the range of IP addresses that resides under that subnet.

By looking at the mask, you can see that up to third octet the mask is 255.255.255, which means the network address will be 172.16.10.0. The 128 in the last octet of the mask indicates that only the first bit of the fourth octet is being used for subnetting, which means there are only two addresses for the subnet ID:

172.16.10.0 and 172.16.10.1

Since the ID 172.16.10.0 is reserved for network ID, the subnet ID is 172.16.10.1.

A subnet mask with 128 in the fourth octet means that only 7 bits are used for the hosts. Therefore, the number of hosts is $2^7 - 2 = 126$.

The broadcast address of this subnet is 172.16.10.01111111=172.16.10.127

Look at the following table to get a detailed explanation of subnets and broadcast address of the IP 172.16.10.5.

	IP addresses	Binary equivalent
Given IP address	172.16.10.5	10101100.00010000.00001010.00000101
Given subnet mask	255.255.255.128	11111111.11111111.11111111.10000000
Network address	172.16.10.0	10101100.00010000.00001010.00000000
Subnet address	172.16.10.128	10101100.00010000.00001010.10000000
Broadcast address	172.16.10.127	10101100.00010000.00001010.01111111
First host address	172.16.10.1	10101100.00010000.00001010.00000001
Second host address	172.16.10.2	10101100.00010000.00001010.00000010
Third host address	172.16.10.3	10101100.00010000.00001010.00000011
…………………	…………………	………………………………………………………………

Last host address	172.16.10.126	10101100.00010000.00001010.0111 1110

Another easy way to find the subnet ID of a given IP address is using the Boolean ANDing operation. The following steps helps to find out the subnet ID from an IP address.

1. Run a bitwise Boolean ANDing between the IP and the given subnet mask to get the subnet ID.

2. After getting the subnet ID, you have to make all host bits 1's to get the broadcast ID for your subnet.

	Binary	IP addresses
Given IP address	10101100.00010000.00001010.000 00101	172.16.10.5
Given subnet mask	11111111.11111111.11111111.10000000	255.255.255.1 28
ANDing the IP and the Mask	10101100.00010000.00001010.000 00000	172.16.10.0

Broadca st address	10101100.00010000.00001010.011 11111	172.16.10.127

Let's take a look at another example

You have an IP address 172.16.7.58 with 27 bits(255.255.255.224) subnet mask. You have to find out the network ID of this IP, and the range of hosts under the network ID.

You can see that the given address is a class B address and the default mask length of class B is 16 bits. The 27-16=11 bits after the first 16 bits (the 11 bits comes from the 8 bits from 3RD octet, and 3 bits from 4TH octet)will be used to represent the subnets. Only the last 5 bits in the 4TH octet are reserved for the host address. Therefore, total number of hosts in each subnet will be 25-2=30

Since we are using the first 3 bits in the fourth octet as subnets, the first subnet will have a host address range from 172.16.7.1 to 172.16.7.31(here we are considering the subnet zero as the first subnet)

The second subnet id will be 172.16.7.32 and this subnet will also have a total of 30 hosts. Therefore the first host address the second subnet is 172.16.7.33 and the last host address is 172.16.7.(32+30)-172.16.7.62. We can see that our given IP falls within the range of second subnet address, which 172.16.7.32.

The broadcast address will always be the next address of the last host address and the address just before the next subnet ID. Can you guess the broadcast address?

The broadcast address 172.16.7.63

How to determine the number of bits to borrow from the hosts for subnetting?

You have a class C address 192.152.19.0 and you need to create a largest possible subnet so that each subnet can have at least 12 hosts. What will be your subnet mask?

Solution: one requirement of the given problem is to have a minimum of 12 hosts in each subnet. Use the 2N-2 formula to calculate the number of bits you need for the host section of your address. Here, n is the number of bits used for host address.

When n=3, you will have 23-2=6 host in each subnet.

When n=4, you will have 24-2=14 host. Since we must have at least 12 hosts in each of our subnet, we need to use four bits for host portion of the IP. That leave us with only 8-4(host bits)=4 bits for subnets.

Thus, total number of subnets will be 24=16

Your mask will look like following:

11111111.11111111.11111111.11110000

255.255.255.240

Subnetting with Class A address

EXAMPLE 1 (mask:255.255.0.0/16)

As you have already seen that the default mask of class A address is 255.0.0.0, which means the only the first 8 bits are used to identify the network and the rest of the 3 octets(24 bits) are used for host address. Suppose, you have a class A address 10.0.0.0 with subnet mask 255.255.0.0 . The subnet mask 255.255.0.0 means that the 8 bits of the second octet will be used to create the subnets.

Total subnets :2$\underline{8}$-2=254. (If you want to use zero subnet and the all-ones or the last subnet, you do not have to subtract 2 from 28, total subnets will be 256)

Total hosts-216-2=65,534

SUBNET ID	First Host	....	Last host	Broadcast ID
10.0.0.0	10.0.0.1	....	10.0.255.254	10.0.255.255
10.1.0.0	10.1.0.1	....	10.1.255.254	10.1.255.255

10.2.0.0	10.2.0.1	....	10.2.255.254	10.2.255.255
....	......	....	....	....
....	.....	....	....	....
10.253.0.0	10.253.0.1		10.253.255.254	10.253.255.255
10.254.0.0	10.254.0.1	....	10.254.255.254	10.254.255.255
10.255.0.0	10.255.0.1	....	10.255.255.254	10.255.255.255

Example 2 (mask :255.255.224.0/19)

For example, we have a subnet mask 255.255.224.0 for a class A network with network ID 10.0.0.0. The /19 means the first 19 bits of the mask will be used for subnet masking. Therefore, total 19-8(class a default mask length is 8)=11 bits are reserved for the subnet ID. And 32-19=13 bits will be used for host ID.

Total subnets: 211-2=2048-2=2046

Total hosts: 213-2=8192-2=8190

When you see that only a portion of an octet is used as a subnet mask or the subnet mask is not 255, you can find the block size of your subnet by subtracting the last octet in the mask from 256. Here, the last octet of the mask is 224. Therefore, the block size of subnet is 256-224=32. The block size indicates the number by which the subnet ID increases. For example, if your first subnet id is 10.0.0.0 and your block size is 32, the first subnet ID is 10.32.0.0 and the next ID will be 10.64.0.0 and so on—always an increment of the block size.

The following table shows the how subnet ID increase by the block size of 32 for a class A network ID 10.0.0.0 with mask 255.255.224.0

SUBNET ID	First Host	...	Last host	Broadcast ID
10.0.0.0	10.0.0.1	...	10.0.31.254	10.0.255.255
10.32.0.0	10.33.0.1	...	10.63.255.254	10.63.255.255
10.64.0.0	10.65.0.1	...	10.95.255.254	10.95.255.255
....	......	...	....	....
....	.....	...	....	....
10.255.160.0	10.255.160.1		10.255.160.254	10.255.160.255

10.255.192.0	10.255.192.1	... .	10.255.192.254	10.254.192.255
10.255.224.0	10.255.224.1	... .	10.255.224.254	10.255.255.255

Subnetting with class B address

If you understand the process involved to subnet a class A address, you will have no difficulty to subnet a class B address because the same process is used to subnet any class of addresses.

Example 1: mask 255.255.192.0 (18 bit)

You have a class B network address (172.16.0.0) and a subnet mask (255.255.192.0). The third octet of the mask is 192, which means the only the first two bits of third octet will be used for subnetting the network.

Network address	172.16.0.0
Subnet mask	255.255.192.0
Total subnets	$2^2-2=2$
Total hosts	$2^{14}-2=16382$
Subnet block size	256-192=64

First subnet or subnet ID	172.16.0.0
Second subnet	172.16.64.0
Third subnet	172.16.128.0
Fourth subnet/broadcast address	172.16.192.0

Since the first subnet id is used as a network ID and the last subnet is used for broadcasting, the usable subnets are 172.16.64.0 and 172.16.128.0

Example 2: mask 255.255.255.128(/25 bit)

You have been given the following class B address with subnet mask 255.255.255.128. Find out the total number of subnets, valid subnets, hosts and broadcast address.

Network address=172.1.0.0

Subnet mask=255.255.255.128

Default mask for class B address is 255.255.0.0 or /16 bit mask. We have been given /25 bit mask. Therefore, we have total 25-16=9 bits to create subnets and

32-25=7 bits to create host addresses.

Total number of subnet=2^9-2=510, if you want to use the first and the last subnet id then the total number of subnets will be 512.

Total number of hosts=2^7-2=126

As you can see for the above diagram that a 25 bit mask (255.255.255.128) in class B address has subnet bits in the 3RD octet and 4TH octet.

The first subnet id will be 172.1.0.0

Subnet id	First host	Second host		Last host	Broadcast address
172.1.0.0	172.1.0.1	172.1.0.2	...	172.1.0.126	172.1.0.127
172.1.0.128	172.1.0.129	172.1.0.130	...	172.1.0.254	172.1.0.255
172.1.1.0	172.1.1.1	172.1.1.2		172.1.1.126	172.1.1.127
172.1.1.128	172.1.1.129	172.1.1.130		172.1.1.254	172.1.1.255
172.1.2.0	172.1.2.1	172.1.2.2		172.1.2.126	172.1.2.127

172.1.2.1 28	172.1.2.1 29	172.1.2.1 30		172.1.2.2 54	172.1.2.2 55
172.1.3. 0	172.1.3.1	172.1.3.2		172.1.3.1 26	172.1.3.1 27
172.1.3.1 28	172.1.3.1 29	172.1.3.1 30		172.1.3.2 54	172.1.3.2 55
--------	---------	---------		-----------	-------
172.1.25 5.0	172.1.25 5.1	172.1.255 .2		172.1.255 .126	172.1.255 .127
172.1.25 5.128	172.1.25 5.129	172.1.255 .130		172.1.255 .254	172.1.255 .255

Example 3: mask 255.255.255.224(27 bit)

You have a subnet mask of 255.255.255.224 for a class B network address 172.16.0.0. Can you guess the number of bits used for subnetting? The 255 in the third octet means that all the 8 bits in that octet are being used for subnetting. And the 224 in the fourth octet means that the first 3 bits of the fourth octet are also used for subnet address. Therefore, total bits used for the subnet are 8+3=11.

Explanation of subnet class B subnet mask 255.255.255.224			
255	255	255	224
11111111	11111111	11111111	11100000
8	8	8	3	5
Default mask length	8+3=11 bits for subnet		5 bits for host

Network address	172.16.0.0	Broadcast address
Subnet mask	255.255.255.224	
Total subnets	211-2=2046	
Total hosts	25-2=30	
Subnet block size	256-224=32	
1st subnet or zero subnet ID	172.16.0.0	172.16.0.31

2nd subnet	172.16.0.32	172.16.0.63
3rd subnet	172.16.0.64	172.16.0.95
4th subnet	172.16.0.96	172.16.0.127
5th subnet	172.16.0.128	172.16.0.159
6th subnet	172.16.0.160	172.16.0.191
7th subnet	172.16.0.192	172.16.0.223
8th subnet	172.16.0.224	172.16.0.255
9th subnet	172.16.1.0	172.16.1.31
10th subnet	172.16.1.32	172.16.1.63
11th subnet	172.16.1.64	172.16.1.95
12th subnet	172.16.1.96	172.16.1.127
13th subnet	172.16.1.128	172.16.1.223
14th subnet	172.16.1.224	172.16.1.255
15th subnet	172.16.2.0	172.16.2.31
16th subnet	172.16.2.32	172.16.2.63
17th subnet	172.16.2.64	172.16.2.95
18th subnet	172.16.2.96	172.16.2.127
....	....	....

....	....	....
....	....	....
	172.16.255.160	172.16.255.191
	172.16.255.192	172.16.255.223
Last subnet	172.16.255.224	172.16.255.255

Questions: Can you find out the first and the last host address of the last subnet of the above example?

Answers: The last subnet address is 172.16.255.224 and its broadcast address is 172.16.255.255. All the numbers in between the subnet ID and the broadcast address are the hosts. Therefore, the first host address is 172.16.255.225 and the last host address is 172.16.255.254

Subnetting with class C address

Suppose, we have a class C network address 192.168.15.0 and a subnet mask 255.255.255.128. The default subnet mask of class C address is 255.255.255.0. The fourth octet in the given mask is 128, which means only the first bit of the fourth octet will be used for subnetting, and the remaining 7 bits will be used for hosts address.

Network ID: 192.168.15.0

Total subnets will be $2^1=2$. The binary equivalent of 128 is 10000000. The number of hosts will be $2^7-2=126$.

The block size of subnet will be 256-128=128, which means every subnet ID will be an increment of 128. If one subnet ID starts at 0, the next subnet ID will start at 128. Since every subnet ID starts with 0, the possible subnet ID will be 192.168.15.0 and 192.168.15.128. The block size 128 also helps to predict the host ID range and the broadcast range. In this example, the starting subnet ID is 192.168.15.0 and its block size is 128, which means the first host id will be 192.168.15.1 (the immediate next IP of the subnet ID) and the broadcast address will be 192.168.15.127.

Subnet ID	192.168.15.0	192.168.15.128
1st host	192.168.15.1	192.168.15.129
2nd host	192.168.15.2	192.168.15.130
3rd host	192.168.15.3	192.168.15.131
4th host	192.168.15.4	192.168.15.132
....	....	....
....	....	....
Last host	192.168.15.126	192.168.15.254

Broadcast ID	192.168.15.127	192.168.15.255

Example 2

Imagine you have a class C address 192.168.20.0 with subnet mask 255.255.255.240.

The binary equivalent of 240 is 11110000, which means only the first four bits are available for subnetting and the remaining four bits for host address.

Total number of subnets: 24=16

Total hosts: 24-2=14

Subnet block size: 256-240=16. The subnets will be 0,16,32,48,64,80,96,112,128,144,160,176,192,208,224,240

Subnet id	First host	Last host	Broadcast address
192.168.20.0	192.168.20.1	192.168.20.14	192.168.20.15
192.168.20.16	192.168.20.17	192.168.20.30	192.168.20.31
192.168.20.32	192.168.20.33	192.168.20.46	192.168.20.47

192.168.20.48	192.168.20.49	192.168.20.62	192.168.20.63
192.168.20.64	192.168.20.65	192.168.20.78	192.168.20.79
192.168.20.80	192.168.20.81	192.168.20.94	192.168.20.95
192.168.20.96	192.168.20.97	192.168.20.110	192.168.20.111
192.168.20.112	192.168.20.113	192.168.20.126	192.168.20.127
192.168.20.128	192.168.20.	192.168.20.142	192.168.20.143
192.168.20.144	192.168.20.145	192.168.20.158	192.168.20.159
192.168.20.160	192.168.20.161	192.168.20.174	192.168.20.175
192.168.20.176	192.168.20.177	192.168.20.190	192.168.20.191
192.168.20.192	192.168.20.193	192.168.20.206	192.168.20.207
192.168.20.208	192.168.20.209	192.168.20.222	192.168.20.223
192.168.20.224	192.168.20.225	192.168.20.238	192.168.20.239
192.168.20.240	192.168.20.241	192.168.20.254	192.168.20.255

Chapter 10. IPv6 Subnetting

In the world of IPv4 subnetting, (as you saw here, it was not as difficult as you thought right?), we had to pay attention to a lot of things that we do not need to concern ourselves with now with IPv6. One of these being the number of hosts we needed. In IPv4 subnetting, we had to make sure that we used the correct subnet mask to segment our network properly and provide enough host for that segment for future growth. Therefore, subnetting in IPv4 sometimes made the network somewhat complex and even more difficult to manage. At least that has been my personal experience.

Now with IPv6 we do not have those concerns, do we? We only pay attention to the Network Prefix of the address, this is the first 64 bits of the address. The /64 is NOT a subnet mask anymore. In IPv6 it's now called a Prefix-length and it deals with the routing process. No longer do we have to worry if we have enough host addresses. This is awesome! I think that speaks for itself don't you think? What I'm trying to convey here is that we no longer have to worry about the Interface ID side of the address.

What throws most people aback with IPv6 addresses and subnetting is the 128 bit address and that it is in hexadecimal format. I know it looks insane, but, "do not fear – Laz is here!" And just like in IPv4 you will use the same method to subnett in IPv6.

You also need to remember that the 4th section of the Network Prefix of an IPv6 address is what has been allotted for you to subnet. This will be the section you will be working with.

Example 1:   2001:3200:1600:**2000**::/51

This is the address you have been given and you must subnet it, into 8 subnets.

How do we attack this problem?

Take the 4th section, which is highlighted in red, and separated into binary format.

2	0	0	0
0010	0000	0000	0000
1st Position	2nd Position	3rd Position	4th Position

Above is how the 2000 would look in its binary format; remember each one of those numbers is comprised of 4 bits that represent a section of 16 bits, which in turn gives us 65,536 networks to work with. By the third section, you have a prefix length of /48.

But wait! You were given a prefix length of /51 as a starting point right? This means, you cannot use anything smaller than /51. This is the starting point for you to subnet in IPv6. Here is where our handy dandy "magic line" comes into play; once you have that taken care of, you then start counting from 49 until you reach 51. Once this is done, you can then begin counting for your eight subnets as shown below:

What you are trying to find is the increment number. In this scenario, it is the bit highlighted in red, which has a value of 4 in the 2nd Position. Therefore, we had to turn on 3 more bits to be able to have 8 subnets which in turn gave us the new Prefix-length of /54.

Let us take a look at how our new subnets would look like:

See...it is the same exact concept as in IPv4. You count for your subnets from left to right and draw your line. The bit value to the left of the line is your network increment, the only difference now is that we increment in Hex.

As you can see in this problem our increment is 4 in the 2nd Position. For that reason, just keep adding 4 to the second number from left to right and that is how you get your values.

The tricky part is that now, you are dealing with letters.

Hex Table

Let's take a look at another example, just to drill it in:

In the following example, your starting address will be the following:

2001:4800:2201:1000::/48.

In this example you were given a prefix-length of /48 and a starting value of 1000. We would like to subnet this address into 6 subnets.

Let's practice one more time!

Once again...below, we are looking for the increment number. Which is the bit value to the left of the line. In this case, that number is 2 in the 1st Position.

Well, there you have it! You needed 6 subnets; so you turned on 3 more bits which now gave you a prefix length of 51. As you can see in the 4th Section you are incrementing by two in the 1st Position.

This is just the tip of the iceberg ladies & gentlemen, there is a lot more to it than this. However, this is the basic fundamentals that you need to know, not only for the CCNA certification exam, but also for hiring purposes. Notice that you can now do it without having to use those weird classical mechanics computations.

> "Laz, will I be asked to subnet in IPv6 for the CCNA exam?" For now, I highly doubt it. But if they do...this book will be your guide to take any IP test with confidence. It is the only IP book you will ever need!

Hex conversions for fun

Let's finish off the book with some easy and fun conversions; especially now that we are using IPv6. Wouldn't it would be fun to learn how to convert hex numbers just for the hell of it? I want you to be an expert in IP's; but would also like you to be familiar with conversions as well. I'm here to tell you that you can count on me for support. ·

Okay now...remember that we have different bases of numbers we use; base 16 which is hex, base 10 which is decimal, and base 2 which is binary. I will show you how you can easily go back and forth from one to the other without complicated formulas.

Below again, are a couple of things you need to know or should already know:

You would add the bit values that are "ON" for each section:

The Hex number would be 94! You would write it in the following format: 0X94.

The "0X" is an identifier to let you know that what you're looking at is a HEX number.

Pretty easy right? It just doesn't get any easier than this!

Let's do a different example.

This time, let's convert a hex number to a decimal: E5

Now you would add the bit values that are "ON" and bring them together as one:

If you add all the bit values that are on...you get a grand total of 229.

That's all there is to it! Just remember to convert first to binary, then to hex or decimal.

You must commit the Hex table, bit values and bit to decimal table to memory. There is no getting around it, if you want to make your life easy - JUST DO IT!

Binary	Bit	Decimal
10000000	1	128
11000000	2	192
11100000	3	224
11110000	4	240
11111000	5	248
11111100	6	252
11111110	7	254
11111111	8	255

Chapter 11. Scaling Networks

When a business gets bigger and more successful, its network requirements also get more complicated. Most businesses depend on network infrastructure when it comes to getting mission-critical services. Oftentimes, outages in the network results in revenue losses and missed customers. This is why network designers should build and design enterprise networks that are available and scalable.

Networks by Design

Say, you are working in a large company and your boss decides to open another branch. One day, your boss tells you that you are being transferred to the office at the new location.

You are a network administrator or network engineer. Your job description includes designing and maintaining networks. Since you have been sent to the new branch, it is now your duty to ensure that the network at that particular location is functional.

Say, the other network administrators in the other branches of your company used the 3-layer hierarchical model. They referred to this model when they designed their networks. Thinking that what they did is such a great approach, you decided to follow suit.

You are now using the very approach that other network administrators are using. You found out that this hierarchical model is helpful in enhancing the designing of networks.

Implementing Network Designs

The Hierarchical Network

Why do you have to scale networks? As you know, businesses continue to expand and depend on the network infrastructures that they have. They do this in order to offer mission-critical services.

When a business continues to expand, it also continues to hire employees and open other branches. In addition, they begin to expand globally. They are no longer just available locally.

Because of these major changes, the network's requirements are significantly affected. Large business environments that have a lot of users, systems, and locations are known as enterprises. The network they use to support their business is known as enterprise network.

Enterprise networks have to support exchanges between network traffic types, including IP telephony, email, and data files. Even video applications have to be supported.

You have to keep in mind that every enterprise network has to do the following:

- It has to support every critical application.

- It has to support converged network traffic.

- It has to support the different trends in business.

- It has to offer a centralized administrative control.

The Business Devices In an Enterprise

Users actually want enterprise networks to always be up and running. In other words, they want these networks to be available and accessible non-stop. In case there is an outage in a network enterprise, the business is no longer able to perform normal tasks. As a result, they may incur a lot of losses in terms of revenue, data, opportunities, and customers.

In order for them to be highly reliable, all enterprise class equipment should be installed in their corresponding enterprise networks. You should take note that enterprise equipment is developed to stricter standards. This makes them better than lower end devices when it comes to moving large amounts of traffic to the network.

The enterprise class equipment has features that make it highly reliable. Some of these features include failover capabilities and redundant power supplies. The failover capability is the ability of the device to go from non-functioning to functioning without any break. For instance, it can switch from being a non-functioning service, device, or module.

If you think that a good network design is no longer necessary when you purchase and install enterprise class equipment, you are wrong. Even if you purchase and install this equipment, you still need to have a network design that is efficient, practical, and functional.

Hierarchical Network Designs

In order for the bandwidth of the enterprise network to be optimized, the network has to stay organized. This is crucial because the traffic has to remain local. It should also avoid being propagated to the other parts of the network when not necessary. If you want to organize your network, you can use the 3-layer hierarchical design model, which divides network functionality into the following layers: access, distribution, and core. Every one of these layers is specifically created for specific functionalities.

For instance, the access layer is there to provide connectivity to users while the distribution layer is necessary for forwarding traffic. Then, there is the core layer, which is a representation of a high-speed backbone layer located between discrete networks.

The access layer is where user traffic gets initiated. Once this is done, the traffic moves through the rest of the layers. Keep in mind that in spite of the three layers featured in the hierarchical model, there are still small enterprise networks that prefer to implement 2-tier hierarchical designs. In 2-tier hierarchical designs, both the distribution and core layers collapse into a single layer. This reduces the complexity and costs involved in the network.

The Cisco Enterprise Architecture

It divides networks into working components and maintains the core, access, and distribution layers at the same time.

The Enterprise Campus

It consists of the whole infrastructure in the campus for the purpose of including access, core, and distribution layers. Switches are available because they provide the port density that you need. In addition, this is where VLAN and trunk link implementation to the distribution layer occur.

You have to take note that it is very important for a building distribution switch to be redundant. Distribution layers often aggregate build access through Layer 3 devices. Access control, QoS, and routing are done at the distribution layer module. Conversely, the core layer is where interconnectivity between the data center server farms, enterprise edge, and distribution layer modules takes place.

Failure Domains

You have to keep in mind that a good network does not only control traffic. It limits the size of the failure domain as well. This is why you have to do your best to design an efficient and functional network. The failure domain is an area of the network that gets affected whenever network servers and critical devices become a problem.

How much impact the failure domain will have relies on the functionality of the device that fails. For instance, if a network segment has a malfunctioning or broken switch, its hosts get affected. Then again, if it is the router, which connects segments to the others, that malfunctions, the network experiences a much greater impact.

In order for a network to minimize its risks of disruption, it has to use reliable enterprise-class equipment as well as redundant links.

A smaller failure domain may lessen the effect of failure on the productivity of the company. Also, it may make troubleshooting much easier. Thus, the downtime for users gets shorter.

Size Limitation for Failure Domains

As you know, failing at the core layer can significantly affect the network. In fact, this impact is so large that network designers tend to focus on preventing failures from occurring in the first place. Then again, doing this also increases the costs involved in implementing their network.

With the hierarchical design model, you will find it easier and cheaper to control failure sizes within the distribution layer. It is in this layer that errors in the network are stored into smaller areas. When this happens, some users get affected. If you use Layer 3 devices on the distribution layer, you will see that the router is able to function as the gateway for several users.

Switch Block Deployment

Multilayer switches or routers tend to be deployed by pair, with the access layer switches divided among them equally. Such configuration is known as switch block, departmental, or building. Every block of switch independently functions, unlike some of the other elements in the network. Because of this, failing no longer causes networks to go down. In the past, when one device fails, the entire network is affected. Then again, the failures of a whole block of switch still do not affect many end users.

Network Expansion

Scalability Designs

In order for you to be able to support enterprise networks, you have to device strategies that allow networks to be scaled and accessed easily and effectively. The following suggestions are ideal for designing basic networks:

You have to make use of expandable and modular equipment, as well as clustered devices if you want to be able to upgrade with ease. These devices or equipment can improve the capabilities of a network. In addition, a device module may be added to existing equipment so that they may be integrated in clusters. The purpose of this is to let them function as a single device and simply the configuration and management of the network.

You have to create a hierarchical network that includes modules. You have to design it in a way that the modules can be upgraded, modified, and added whenever necessary. When doing this, the design of other working areas should not be affected in any way. For instance, you can create an access layer that may be expanded without having any impact on the core and distribution layers of the network.

You have to create IPv6 and IPv4 addresses in a strategical sense. See to it that you carefully plan for your IPv4 addresses. If you do this, there would no longer be any need for network re-addressing. You may support added services and users with ease.

You have to select multilayer switches and routers carefully. Make sure that they are able to limit broadcasts as well as filter out unwanted traffic. You can make use of Layer 3 devices when filtering and reducing the traffic that goes to the core of the network.

You have to implement redundant links in your network. You should do this between the core and access layer devices and the critical devices.

You have to implement numerous links between your equipment. You can have an equal cost load balancing or link aggregation to improve your bandwidth. You should also combine all the Ethernet links into just one EtherChannel configuration. If you do this, you increase your available bandwidth. In addition, it is much more practical and cost effective to use an EtherChannel because fiber runs and high speed interfaces are very expensive.

You have to implement wireless connectivity in order for you to allow for expansion and mobility.

You have to make use of scalable routing protocols as well as implement the features of these particular routing protocols. The main objective here is to isolate the routing updates as well as reduce the routing table size.

Redundancy Planning

Redundancy Implementation

For a lot of organizations and companies, network availability is crucial for supporting their business needs. Why is redundancy important? Well, it is a vital part of your network design because it is greatly helpful when it comes to preventing network service disruptions. It also minimizes the chances of a single point of failure occurring. One of the methods you can use to implement redundancy is to install duplicate equipment. You can also give critical devices failover services.

You can also implement redundancy by using redundant paths. These paths actually provide an alternative to the physical paths that data in the network use to get around. The redundant paths within a switched network are supportive of high availability. Then again, because of switch operations, the redundant paths within switched Ethernet networks become prone to causing logical Layer 2 loops. In times like this, you may need to use a Spanning Tree Protocol (STP).

The STP gets rid of the Layer 2 loops each time a redundant link is used in between switches. You will notice that it does this by offering a mechanism for a redundant path within a switched network. It keeps on doing this until it needs a path. STP is also an open standard protocol, which is used in switched environments in order to develop a logical topology without any loops.

Bandwidth Increase

EtherChannel Implementation

In a hierarchical network design, there are some links that have to have more traffic than the others. As traffic coming from multiple links comes together into a single and outgoing link, it becomes possible for this link to be a bottleneck.

As an administrator, you are allowed to raise the number of bandwidths between the devices you use. You can create a single logic link that consists of a few physical links. One form of link aggregation is EtherChannel. It is used for switched networks.

The EtherChannel makes use of existing switch ports. As a result, there is no more need for added costs for upgrades. You no longer need to pay for a better connection. You can enjoy a fast connection without any hassle. In addition, configuring the

EtherChannel is all about load balancing in between the links of EtherChannel itself, and then relying on the platform of the hardware.

Access Layer Expansion

Wireless Connectivity Implementation

You need to design your network in a way that you are able to make your network access expand. Keep in mind that wireless connectivity is actually one of the most important aspects of extending layer connectivity. Through this strategy, you can have more flexibility, ability to adapt to different environments, and reduced costs.

In order for end devices to be able to communicate wirelessly, there has to be a wireless NIC, which involves the use of a radio transmitter or receiver. It should also incorporate studio transmitters and receivers as well as their software drivers. Without any wireless access point (AP) or wireless router, you will not be able to connect.

Anyway, there are plenty of things you need to consider when it comes to wireless network implementation. For instance, you should see to it that certain types of devices are used. You should also factor in interface considerations, security considerations, and wireless coverage requirements.

Fine-Tuning the Routing Protocols

Routed Network Management

Due to the frequencies of which ISPs and networks are used, link-state protocols have started to be used for advanced protocols.

OSPF

The Open Shortest Path First (OSPF) is a link-state routing protocol. It is great for large hierarchical networks in which quick convergence is necessary. In addition, OSPF routers built and maintained neighbor adjacency. With it, every link state update is sent whenever there are changes in the network.

Chapter 12.   How to Secure Your Network

The security of your network should not be taken for granted but should be of paramount importance to you. It is imperative that you put preventive measures in place to forestall both external and internal attacks on your network. Consider these security measures:

Update your patches

Cybercriminals are reputable for exploiting vulnerability in software applications, operating systems, browser plug-ins, and web browsers. Thus, to prevent cybercriminals from exploiting the vulnerability, ensure that you use the latest software applications. If your software applications have automatic updating feature, enable this. You should also take an inventory of your hardware as well. Pay attention to the hardware and other devices connected to the network. Are they the latest versions with the right protection? Can they withstand attacks or will they cave in under pressure and thus serve as the loophole that will be exploited?

The updated versions of these applications and hardware are designed to rectify some of the loopholes in outdated versions that can be exploited by cyber attackers. This includes fixing bugs and other potential weaknesses in the applications. Malicious programs such as worms, Trojans, viruses, and other harmful malware are created regularly. As they are created, they are equally designed to adapt to existing security ensures and exploit any weaknesses and loopholes in system software. Thus, any existing security system implemented in your network may be effective against current malware programs. Thus, you are guaranteed by using applications that can withstand potential hackings.

Configure your exception handling processes

There may be some error messages when your network is in operation. How you handle the errors may also have a bearing on the security of your network. A practical tip is to configure your network's exception handling processes to ensure that whatever error message that is generated is returned to the external or internal system. It may also involve preventing users from including sensitive information that attackers may find useful.

Conduct assurance processes

Your security measure should include conducting assurance processes. To do this, you must regularly conduct penetration tests of your network's architecture as well as perform simulated cyber-attacks on the network with a view to ensure that your network can withstand attacks.

Use strong passwords

Passwords are integral parts of a network. A couple of network components and software are usually password-protected for obvious reasons. However, passwording a component or software doesn't guarantee protection against hacking if you don't do it right. Passwording your network or its components goes beyond using random words. There are some useful tips that will help you create a very formidable and strong password for your network. Here are some tips:

- It should be long: This is one of the areas where a lot of people expose themselves to attacks. Out of their desire to make their passwords easy to remember, they use very short, easy-to-remember passwords. Therein lies the problem. If your password is very short and can easily be remembered, chances are that they are pretty easy to crack as well. According to cybersecurity experts, the difficulty of cracking passwords is directly proportional to the length and complexity of the password. For instance, consider these two passwords:

Password A: mynetwork
Password B: @Mypassword&2018

It is very obvious that hackers will be delighted to have to deal with Password A due to its short length and other factors noted below.

- It should contain alphanumeric characters: Well, this is a valuable tip that shouldn't be ignored. A strong password is not made of alphabets alone but a mixture of both alphabets and numbers, hence, alphanumeric. When you compare Password A and Password B, it is pretty obvious that the former is made up of alphabets only while the latter is a combination of alphabets and some numbers. The inclusion of the numbers increases the strength of the password and forms a more difficult to hack password.

- Include special characters: I'm of the opinion that you understand what a special character is. These are characters like @, $, &, !, and ^ to present a few. To increase your password strength, you should include some of these special characters in your password. They also contribute to the strength of the password, a deterrent to potential hackers. In the case study above, Password A doesn't include a single special character. That makes the user of such password a sitting duck, vulnerable to attacks. It will only take hackers a couple of minutes to circumvent the password and gain unauthorized access to the network. In sharp contrast, Password B contains some special characters such as @

and &. This makes the password stronger than its counterpart. In a nutshell, Password B ticks all the boxes – is longer, contains special characters, and is alphanumeric — and is a stronger password than Password A.

- Change your password regularly: According to the SANS Institute, passwords should be changed regularly. The institute recommends changing your password at least every 3 months to make it difficult for people to monitor your password.

- Don't reuse passwords: Reusing passwords is the greatest undoing of many people that have fallen victim of hacking. The danger lies in getting access to one of your passwords and the hacker will take over the entire network within a short time. The institute also suggests that you shouldn't reuse your last 15 passwords.

- Don't share your password(s) indiscriminately: If you have the habit of sharing your password(s) to every Tom, Dick, and Harry, that may turn out to be your undoing. You obviously have no idea of who will use the password for malicious intent, thereby harming both you and your network. Thus, unless it is absolutely necessary, you shouldn't share your password(s) with anyone. If you have to do it, ensure you are sharing with people with a track record of integrity, not someone with a huge question mark over his or her integrity.

- Set up guest network access: If you must allow visitors and friends access to your network, it is a course of wisdom to create a guest network access for them. That allows you to give them a different password from the administrator's password at your disposal. This prevents users with malicious intent from gaining unauthorized administrator's access.

- Consider using password manager: A password manager can serve as a reliable storage place for your password, especially if you are using a password that is so difficult and strong that you can't easily remember it. Rather than store passwords on one of the connected devices where they can easily be stolen, a password manager is safe and easy to use.

If you want a convenient way of remembering your network password, the password manager is the right tool. You only need to remember the password to the manager. Once you unlock your account, all the previously saved passwords on the account become accessible, and you won't have to always keep a long list of passwords in unsafe places. Password managers come in three different types: online password manager services, password manager software, and password manager apps for Android and iPhone users.

Some free Android password managers are Secrets for Android and KeePassDroid. If you are an iPhone user, you have Passible, Dashlane, 1Password, and LastPass to choose from. Each of these password managers has its pros and cons that should be given much consideration before settling for it. Thus, you should do your due diligence when shopping for a password manager so you can get the password manager that meets your personal needs. A visit to the official websites of these managers will give you the information you need.

When creating passwords for your network and its components, always keep these tips in mind. This will assist you to create formidable passwords that will boost the security of your network. Sometimes, creating a password can be very challenging. You may have to struggle with the challenge of how to combine these tips to create the perfect passwords for your network without relying on random passwords. Just as there are tips that are valuable in creating strong passwords, there are also some tips that remove the stress of creating a password and makes the process pretty easy. Let's consider a few of these tips:

- Don't turn to the dictionary for your choice of word. As a rule of thumb, don't use any dictionary word. Potential hackers are literate too that use sophisticated tools that can easily pick any dictionary word used as a password.

- Avoid foreign words and proper nouns as well. You can do better than rely on these words and nouns. Remember, they have the right tools for their jobs and can easily detect these words.

- Avoid using numbers that can easily be guessed if a hacker takes a look at your email. Numbers that are derived from your date of birth, street numbers, phone numbers, social security number, and other personal information shouldn't be a part of your password. You put yourself at a great risk if you include these numbers. A peep into your email content may give you away.

- You should also avoid using anything that is remotely or closely related to your nickname, name, pets, and family members. If you use words from the list above and the hackers have access to them, reaching you won't pose a challenge.

- What about choosing a phrase you can identify with? Using phrases that have meaning for you can be of help too. Make a list of these phrases and take the first word of the phrases to come up with something unique that can't be easily guessed.

When you implement these tips, you will come up with a unique password. Then, add some special characters and numbers to the newly-coined word, and you have a unique, strong, and difficult to crack a password.

Secure your VPN

You can secure your VPN by paying attention to identity authentication and data encryption. If you keep your network connection open, you are giving hackers a vulnerability they can easily exploit to take over your network. What is more, the vulnerability of data increases as it travels over the Internet. Thus, it is important that you review the appropriate documentation for your VPN software and server to ensure that you are not using anything but the strongest protocol for authentication and encryption. Another brilliant idea is to separate your VPN network from the other parts of the network with a firewall. Thus, an attack on your network won't have any impact on your VPN.

You should also consider these tips:

- Create some user-access policies and enforce them.

- Make sure that people connected to the network can handle the security of their wireless networks without issues. Malicious software programs that have infected their devices may also infect the network if not properly handled.

- You should always check the firewalls and other security measures you put in place regularly to ensure that they are up-to-date and still effective.

If it is a company network, the following security measures will be valuable to the company:

- Compile a list of authorized software and don't allow your employees to downloading applications that are not on the list. With the assistance of software inventory applications, you can get the list.

- If the company has written security policies, update them regularly. For instance, spell out the personal devices that are allowed to have access to the network. Don't forget to state specifically how long a device should be stolen or lost before it is reported.

- You should also run vulnerability scanning tools once a week.

- Don't forget to monitor your network traffic. This will allow you to notice possible threats and unusual activity patterns that can be prevented with the right approach.

Implement Access Control

It is important to know that not every Tom, Dick, and Harry should have unrestricted access to your network. The goal is to ensure that you have control of those who have access to the network. This is very important if you wish to keep potential attackers out of your network. If you can't recognize each device and user, your chances of being attacked will increase. With this knowledge, it becomes easier for you to enforce any security policies you have put in place. You can equally block or give limited access to noncompliant endpoint devices as a way of monitoring access to the network.

Data loss prevention

This is absolutely important if you are running a company or an organization. You should put a measure in place that will drastically prevent data loss. A practical solution is to prevent your staff from sending sensitive information that may be used against you by hackers outside the network. You can take the preventive measure a bit further by installing DLP (Data Loss Prevention) technologies. These technologies are effective at stopping people from forwarding, uploading, or printing sensitive information without authorization. Thus, rest assured that the security of your data is guaranteed and that will also prevent data loss through any of the channels listed above.

The importance of this technology to the security of your network cannot be overemphasized. Sensitive data and information can end up in the wrong hands through instant messaging, email, file transfers, website forms, and other channels. With DLP strategies, you have an effective solution that can monitor the flow of information with a view to detect and block an unauthorized flow of information from the network.

DLP technologies work on a set of rules that allow them to search through electronic communications in search of sensitive information or to detect any abnormal data transfers in the network. Some of the valuable pieces of information that can be prevented from leaving the network include financial data, intellectual property, customer details, and other pieces of information that may be either intentionally or accidentally leaked. There are different DLP technologies for a variety of uses too. These are:

- DLP for data in use: This DLP class is effective for securing in use. This is data that an endpoint or an application is actively processing. The safeguards used here involve controlling users' access to some resources as well as authenticating users.

- DLP for data in motion: Sometimes, confidential data may be in transit across a network and may need to be protected in transit. This technology is needed to ensure that the data is not routed to an insecure storage area or outside the organization. One of the most effective technologies used to achieve this is encryption. Email security also plays a huge part here.

- DLP for data at rest: You equally need to protect a data at rest just as you deem it fit to pay attention to other data. This DLP technology is designed for protecting data residing in different storage mediums such as a cloud. DLP can effectively control access and track such data.

Use antimalware and antivirus software

Malware is a shortened form of malicious software. This includes worms, viruses, ransomware, and the likes. Sometimes, a network may be infected by malware without visible impact due to the ability of malware to lie dormant for a couple of days or weeks before attacking the network. In the dormant state, it plans how to attack your network and will eventually carry out its plans if it is not swiftly identified and removed.

With the best antimalware programs, you can scan your network for malware upon entry, and it prevents the entry of any malware spotted during the scan. In addition, the program will continuously scan your network for potential dangers, anomalies, and whatever can compromise the security of the network.

Wireless security

It is a known fact that wireless networks don't boast of the same security that wired networks can boast of. If you don't put some stringent security measures in place, using a wireless network will expose you to hacking. To prevent the security weakness of your wireless network to be exploited, it is important that you fortify your network security with products that are specifically designed for protecting wireless networks.

An effective wireless security solution will guarantee:

- Rogue detection that will effectively prevent any attempt to breach the security of your network by opening unsecured holes in it

- Continuous analysis of your wireless spectrum's quality

- Scanning for mitigation and threat detection

These attributes give you the confidence that your network and other devices connected to it are well protected.

Network Segmentation

Network segmentation is a software-defined security technology for classifying network traffic into different categories. This makes it easier for you to enforce security policies on those using the network. This classification is based on the endpoint entity and not the mere IP addresses only. The access can be assigned based on location, role, and other factors so that the right users receive the right access level while suspicious devices are prevented from gaining access to the network, making it easy to remediate the problem.

Intrusion Prevention System

Using an Intrusion Prevention System (IPS) is a good way to give your network top-notch security. The system is designed to scan network traffic with the objective of blocking attacks. One of the best of these prevention systems is the Cisco Next-Generation system. It correlates global threat intelligence and uses the knowledge to block all malicious activities on a network in addition to tracking how suspect malware and files move across the network in order to prevent the spread of outbreaks and thus prevent reinfection as well.

Email security

Email gateways are the most popular tool for a security breach. For years, attackers have mastered the act of using social engineering tactics and personal information for building sophisticated and effective phishing campaigns for deceiving recipients and eventually hacking their networks. You have tons of email security applications at your disposal. These applications can block incoming attacks and prevent them from wreaking havoc on your network. They are also effective for controlling outbound messages, another preventive measure against the loss of confidential and sensitive data.

Web Security

The significance of a web security solution to your network security cannot be ignored. The right solution will control how your staff use the web, block potential threats, and generally deny them access to malicious websites. Whether you have your web gateway in the cloud or on site, the web security solution will also protect it.

Application Security

It is imperative that you protect whatever software you run on your network. Regardless of whether the software is purchased from a third party or developed by your IT staff, ensure that they are well protected as a preventive measure against being made vulnerable to attacks by the software. For instance, it is not strange to detect vulnerabilities or holes in software programs, and hackers won't hesitate to exploit that loophole. Thus, application security includes the software, hardware, and other processes you deployed to block potential holes that can be used against your network.

Behavioral Analytics

I once mentioned the importance of monitoring your network for signs of anomalies or irrational behavior on the network. However, this won't be possible if you have no idea what constitutes irrational behavior or what it looks like. You don't have to stress yourself thinking about how to go about it or identify abnormal behaviors. You have some effective tools, such as behavioral analytics tools, at your disposal. These tools will automatically scan your network for irregular activities that deviate from the norm. Then, your security team can take over by identifying the threat and quickly addressing it.

Consider physical network security

This basic security measure is most at times overlooked. This technique involves keeping your network hardware well protected from physical intrusion or theft. You should know that corporations don't joke with this security measure because it is quite effective regardless of how simple it is. They spend huge sums of money to create well-guarded facilities where they lock their network switches, network servers, and other important network components.

Well, if you have your network at home or other small places, building a separate compartment for locking them up may be out of the equation. However, you can still implement this security measure. Keep your broadband routers in well-guarded and safe private locations in your home. Those places should be kept secret from guests and nosy neighbors. If you are concerned about physical theft, an effective solution is not storing your data locally. You can use online backup services for keeping sensitive files stored in safe locations that ensure the security of your data if your local hardware is compromised or stolen.

As a part of the physical network security measure, pay attention to how you use your mobile devices, especially if they are connected to a network; it is very easy to leave small gadgets behind when using them in public places or have them fall out of your pockets ignorantly. There are stories abound of people who have their smartphone and other mobile devices stolen in public. In some cases, these devices were stolen while being used. Thus, it is important that you are alert to your environment when using mobile devices.

Finally, monitor your phone whenever you loan it to someone. This precautionary measure is important because a malicious person can install monitoring software on the phone, steal your personal data, or conduct some other harmful activities that may compromise the integrity of your network if you leave him unattended for a couple of minutes. The combination of two or more of these security techniques will increase the security of your network and thus prevent the network from sudden and destructive attacks. This will ensure the continuous use of the network without the fear of losing valuable and sensitive information or data to unauthorized personnel.

Wireless Network Security

A decade ago, computers were considered as a luxury and not a necessity. It was the exclusive property of the wealthy and lucky and a network was exclusively reserved for large organizations and corporations. However, things have changed. Nearly everyone now has access to a computer or some other Internet-enabled devices. Wireless networking technology has really made a network available for all and sundry. However, this comes at a price: insecurity. Your network can be remotely hacked while your confidential information may be stolen for a ransom (ransomware) or for some other purposes. However, with some security measures, you can fortify your wireless network's security issues and prevent hackers from exploiting you. Consider these tips:

- Disable identifier broadcasting: Of course, you increase your chances of getting hacked if you announce to the world that you have a wireless connection. Trust hackers to pay you an unscheduled visit. Therefore, it is an invitation to disaster if you keep your identifier broadcasting enabled. Increase your network security by disabling this feature. Check your hardware's manual to enable you to disable this feature and secure your network.

- Restrict unnecessary traffic: Many wireless and wired routers are equipped with built-in firewalls designed to provide a line of defense for your network. In order to understand how to take advantage of this simple security measure, read your hardware's manual and learn the best way to configure your router to give access to approved outgoing and incoming traffic only.

Combine these security measures with the ones discussed previously, and you have a solid and formidable network that can't easily be hacked.

Conclusion

You are embarking on a journey that will get you so far, and change your life. The lessons you learn in this book will help you go a long way in your career as a networking expert. Once you are done reading this book, set aside some time and think about everything you have read. Each chapter offers useful information, and pointers that will guide you.

One of the important things you need in networking is a practice lab, or a computer on which you can try your hands on some of the lessons you learn in this book. The world of networking is advancing and keeps developing over time. Some conventions might change in a few years. With this in mind, therefore, try and make sure you have access to some practice material to help you stay abreast with technologies in networking.

If you have been in the corporate space for a long time, you will realize that staffing managers today focus more on applications over papers. You might have some really awesome papers but if you are unable to apply the knowledge learned and solve problems for the manager, they would not see the benefit of hiring you for the job.

There is so much you can learn about networks and how to manage them effectively. At the moment, network security is one of the biggest concerns that a lot of organizations grapple with. You are expected to know how to deal with this. When hired, the decision makers in your organization believe that you have what it takes to protect and safeguard their network resources.

The beauty of computing today is that there is so much evolution taking place. Things change so fast, yet somehow they remain the same. With in-depth knowledge of CompTIA Network+ you learn important lessons that will help you advance and evolve with technological advances as they happen.

www.ingramcontent.com/pod-product-compliance
Lightning Source LLC
Chambersburg PA
CBHW071137050326
40690CB00008B/1487